Sri Guru

AF668112

SPEAK ENGLISH AT SCHOOL

Name : ....

Class : ....

Sec : ....

Roll No. : ....

YouTube Channel: Sri Guru Academy

TITLE OF THE BOOK	:	**SPEAK ENGLISH AT SCHOOL**
AUTHOR	:	**Thanga Durai** M.A M.Phil.,
FIRST EDITION	:	2019
SECOND EDITION	:	2025
PAGES	:	200
PRICE	:	**250**
ISBN NUMBER	:	978-81-995468-8-2
CONTACT NUMBER	:	7530008201
EMAIL ID	:	srigurupub@gmail.com
PUBLISHER (Imprint)	:	**Sri Guru Publication** Madurai.
PRINTER	:	**Sri Meenakshi Printers** Madurai.

CLASSROOM RULES

- Come to school regularly.
- Arrive on time.
- Enter / leave the classroom quietly.
- Be ready to learn.
- Be active in the classroom.
- Be responsible.
- Be attentive.
- Focus on your work.
- Listen to the teacher carefully.
- Bring your books and notebooks.
- Raise your hand to speak.
- Say ‘please’ and ‘thank you’.
- Use appropriate language.
- Listen when others are speaking.
- Complete assignments on time.
- Leave the excuses at the door.
- Tell the truth.
- Ask for help when you need it.
- Learn from your mistakes.
- Keep your hands, feet and things to yourself.
- Return the things to their proper places.
- Keep your room clean and tidy.
- Respect the teacher, classmates and school property.
- Work and play in a safe manner.
- Stay away from off limit classroom areas.
- Do not bring mobile phone.
- Do not disturb others.
- Do not hit anyone.
- Do not shout in the classroom.
- Do not talk when the teacher is talking.
- Tell someone if you are being bullied or threatened.

- Follow the school rules.
- Gaining the knowledge is important.
- Never stop trying.
- See failure as a beginning, not an end.
- Have a positive attitude.
- Encourage each other.
- Forgive others.
- Believe in yourself.

By the same Author:

- Spoken English (English – Tamil)
- Spoken English for Police and Advocate (Eng-Tam)
- English In Business Field And It Sector
- Speak English at School
- Learn to Speak English
- Basic Question Answers for Communication
- Basic Conversation
- 6000 Important Vocabulary for Life
- 1500 Children's Vocabulary

S.No.	CONTENTS	Page No.

1. SELF-INTRODUCTION

- My name is Arun.
- I am John.
- I am 10 years old.
- My age is 12.
- I am studying 9th standard.
- I am studying in Royal Matriculation Hr. Sec. School.
- I am studying 8th standard in Sadhana Hr. Sec. School.
- I come from K.K.Nagar.
- I am coming from S.S.Colony.
- My father's name is Ashwin.
- He is a Teacher.
- He is working in a private company.
- My mother's name is Sheela.
- She is a homemaker.
- She is a Manager in a private company.
- There are five members in our family.
- I have two brothers and a sister.
- I have two sisters.
- I am the only child.
- I have an elder brother and sister.
- I have two brothers, one older and one younger.
- I have a brother. His name is Kamal.
- He is studying 8th standard.
- My hobby is reading.
- My hobbies are reading, listening music, and playing chess.
- My aim is to become a Scientist.

2. SCHOOL LANGUAGE

FOR ***STUDENTS***

- Hi.
- Hello.
- Good morning.
- Good afternoon.
- Good evening.
- How are you?
- I am fine.
- What is your name?
- My name is Rahul.
- Nice to meet you.
- How old are you?
- I am ten years old.
- Which class are you in?
- I am in class five.
- Where do you live?
- I live in Mumbai.
- Can I sit here?
- Please help me.
- Thank you.
- You are welcome.
- Sorry.
- Excuse me.
- Please come here.
- Please wait.
- Let us go.
- Come with me.

- Sit down.
- Stand up.
- Open your book.
- Close your book.
- Read this line.
- Write your name.
- Listen carefully.
- Speak slowly.
- This is my book.
- That is your bag.
- Where is my pencil?
- I need an eraser.
- Can I borrow your pen?
- Here is your pen.
- Thank you very much.
- What is today's homework?
- Which page is this?
- Turn the page.
- I am ready.
- I finished my work.
- I need more time.
- This question is easy.
- This question is difficult.
- Please help me with this sum.
- I like English.
- I like mathematics.
- My favourite subject is science.
- I like drawing.
- I like reading books.

- Let us study together.
- Let us play together.
- Can you teach me?
- I will try again.
- Good job.
- Well done.
- Congratulations.
- Best of luck.
- Do not worry.
- Keep trying.
- I am happy.
- I am sad.
- I am tired.
- I am hungry.
- I am thirsty.
- I feel better now.
- I like this game.
- This is interesting.
- I enjoyed the class.
- Please be quiet.
- The teacher is coming.
- Class is starting.
- Class is over.
- Let us clean the classroom.
- Please switch on the fan.
- Please switch off the light.
- Open the window.
- Close the door.
- Keep your bag here.

- This is my seat.
- Please move a little.
- Can I join your group?
- Let us do the project.
- We are friends.
- He is my friend.
- She is my classmate.
- We study in the same class.
- I like my school.
- Our school is big.
- Our classroom is clean.
- I go to school every day.
- I come by bus.
- I walk to school.
- I brought my lunch.
- Let us eat together.
- The food is tasty.
- I need some water.
- Please give me the bottle.
- I will return it tomorrow.
- What time is it?
- It is lunch time.
- It is break time.
- It is time to go home.
- See you tomorrow.
- Bye.
- Take care.
- Have a nice day.
- I can read English.

- I can write English.
- I can speak English.
- I want to learn more.
- I practice every day.
- Reading is fun.
- Writing is easy.
- I like to sing songs.
- I can dance well.
- I like sports.
- Cricket is my favourite game.
- I play football.
- We won the match.
- Our team played well.
- Let us practice again.
- I have a new bag.
- Your shoes are nice.
- I like your drawing.
- This is beautiful.
- Please show me your notebook.
- My answer is correct.
- I made a mistake.
- Please correct me.
- I understand now.
- I am learning fast.
- Can you say that again?
- Please write clearly.
- I need a sharpener.
- My pen is not working.
- I lost my ruler.

- I found your book.
- Here it is.
- Let us stand in a line.
- Walk slowly.
- Do not run.
- Be careful.
- Keep the classroom clean.
- Throw the paper in the dustbin.
- Please share your notes.
- I missed the class yesterday.
- I was absent yesterday.
- I came early today.
- I am excited.
- Today is my birthday.
- Thank you for your wishes.
- I brought chocolates.
- Let us celebrate.
- I like school activities.
- I enjoy group work.
- We are a good team.
- Let us help each other.
- Practice makes perfect.
- Hard work is important.
- I want to become a doctor.
- I want to become a teacher.
- I want to become an engineer.
- I love my parents.
- My mother helps me study.
- My father goes to work.

- I help my parents at home.
- I wake up early.
- I do my homework daily.
- I respect my teachers.
- I respect my elders.
- Time is very important.
- I will do my best.
- I believe in myself.
- I can do it.
- Never give up.
- Keep smiling.
- Thank you everyone.
- Do you have an extra pen?
- Can I borrow your notebook?
- What is today's homework?
- Did you understand the lesson?
- Let us study together.
- Can you explain this question?
- I missed yesterday's class.
- Please share your notes.
- Are you ready for the test?
- Which subject do you like most?
- I like your handwriting.
- Can we work in a group?
- Please speak softly.
- Let us go to the library.
- Did you complete the project?
- I need your help with maths.
- That answer is correct.

- I think you are right.
- Let us ask the teacher.
- Can you repeat that?
- I did not hear properly.
- What page are we on?
- Please wait for me.
- Let us practice English.
- You did a great job.
- Congratulations on your result.
- I enjoyed today's activity.
- Can you teach me this chapter?
- I forgot my homework.
- Please remind me tomorrow.
- Let us prepare for the exam.
- I am nervous about the test.
- Do not worry, you can do it.
- Shall we revise together?
- Your drawing looks nice.
- Can I join your team?
- Let us play after school.
- What did the teacher say?
- Please move a little.
- I think this answer is wrong.
- Can we discuss this topic?
- I need more practice.
- You are improving a lot.
- I respect your opinion.
- Thank you for helping me.
- Sorry, I made a mistake.

- Please forgive me.
- I appreciate your support.
- Let us complete the assignment.
- Which chapter will come in the exam?
- Did you study for tomorrow?
- I am feeling sleepy today.
- Can you wake me up tomorrow?
- Let us participate in the competition.
- You speak English very well.
- I want to improve my grammar.
- Can you check my answers?
- Let us ask doubts together.
- I think this lesson is easy.
- This question is confusing.
- We should submit the work today.
- Please do not copy my answers.
- Let us be friends.
- I learned something new today.
- You explained it very clearly.
- I am happy to work with you.
- Can we exchange books?
- Please keep quiet.
- The teacher is coming.
- Let us hurry up.
- Did you bring your lunch?
- I forgot my water bottle.
- Let us clean the classroom.
- Your idea is creative.
- I need your opinion.

- Let us solve this together.
- Can you save a seat for me?
- I am excited about the trip.
- Please share the information.
- I could not solve this problem.
- Let us ask seniors for help.
- You are very talented.
- Keep practicing every day.
- I trust your answer.
- Let us attend the seminar.
- We should respect everyone.
- I am proud of our team.
- Can you send me the notes?
- Please message me later.
- I enjoyed talking with you.
- Let us focus on studies.
- We can do better next time.
- Never give up.
- Best of luck for the exam.
- See you tomorrow.
- Can you tell me about yourself?
- This is Kamal. He is studying with me.
- This is my friend David.
- I want to introduce my friend. He is Arjun.
- You are welcome to join us.
- Where is your home?
- Where do you come from?
- Which is your native place?
- My native place is Chennai.

- I am from K.K.Nagar.
- How old are you?
- I am 14 years old.
- She is 10 years old.
- Do you have any brothers or sisters?
- I do not have any brothers and sisters.
- I am the only child.
- Who is she?
- This is my cousin, Shreya.
- She is my mother-in-law.
- Who is he?
- He is my grandfather.
- He is my younger brother.
- Do you live around here?
- I live with my parents.
- I live in my aunt's house.
- He is a tidy person.
- Our school starts at 8:30 a.m.
- Are you ready?
- Are you ready to go to school?
- Yes, I am ready.
- Where is Nisha?
- I am here.
- Here I am.
- Please hurry.
- Why are you in hurry?
- Hurry up! You will miss your school bus.
- If you don't hurry, you will miss the van.
- Let's go, it is time.

- Come on, It is too late.
- I am running late.
- Sit beside me.
- We arrived at school late.
- Did you come late?
- I couldn't make it.
- You didn't come to the class that day.
- How much pocket money do your parents give you?
- What class you study?
- In which class are you studying?
- May I come in?
- I am sorry, I am late.
- Thank you, sir.
- My lunch time is at noon.
- Give me my bag.
- Where is my note?
- Where is your book?
- It is on the table.
- It is in the drawer.
- The book is behind the table.
- The book is near the table.
- It is above the desk.
- It is to the left of the desk.
- It is between the boxes.
- The book is next to the desk.
- It is in front of the table.
- It is under the desk.
- It is over the door.
- It is opposite to the box.

- There is a book under the table.
- See for yourself.
- I need your help.
- Where can I get textbooks?
- Can you help me buy my textbooks?
- Could you pass me the book please?
- Close the door.
- I can't close the door.
- The door is stuck.
- I am thirsty.
- May I drink water?
- I feel hungry.
- I want an eraser.
- Where are you?
- I am coming.
- Who are you looking at?
- What are you looking for?
- I lost my note.
- My pen is different from that.
- I cannot find my pen.
- If it is not yours, ask before you use it.
- I got a haircut.
- Where are you going?
- I am going to physics lab.
- Shall we go for a walk?
- What are you doing?
- I am writing.
- I am studying.
- I am playing.

- Where is she?
- She is coming.
- What is she doing?
- She is writing.
- She is playing.
- He is crying.
- What are they doing?
- Where are they?
- They are fighting.
- They are playing in the ground.
- What is he doing?
- He is reading.
- Who beat you?
- It's him.
- It's not him.
- Your shirt is missing a button.
- So what?
- Your bag is beautiful.
- It has holes.
- I didn't see it.
- Oh, here it is.
- Let me go!
- Let me see that.
- Let's see what happen.
- Let's go to my house.
- Let's be ready.
- Let's go to the restroom.
- Let me go and see what is wrong.
- Please, let me come in.

- Let's try.
- Whose pencil is this?
- I do not know. It is not mine.
- This is mine not yours.
- Whose pen is this?
- It's mine.
- It is not mine.
- It's hers.
- Are you sure?
- Make sure.
- Do you have pencil?
- Yes, I have.
- Not a problem, here it is!
- What is this?
- What will you do at home?
- The book is covered with dust.
- Take it out.
- He is very lazy.
- Tell me about your parents.
- My father is very strict.
- My mother is friendly.
- May I go out, please?
- May I go to toilet / restroom?
- I should go to the toilet very soon.
- Madam, I really want to go to the toilet.
- Shall I go home?
- Shall I come?
- What did I do?
- I didn't do, sir.

- I am ready, may I start now?
- I am next.
- I have a book in my bag.
- Can I go to the board?
- What page is it, please?
- The teacher is teaching Science.
- How do you pronounce?
- Is he a teacher?
- Is it right?
- Yes, it is right.
- Is this ok?
- Tomorrow is the first day of school.
- Is this correct?
- Is it useful?
- Yes, it is useful.
- Is the van coming?
- Yes, it is coming.
- She is not my type.
- Don't advise me on anything.
- Is she waiting for you?
- Yes, she is waiting for me.
- I have to teach her a lesson.
- Is it purple?
- Is this blue?
- Yes, it is blue.
- No, it is not blue.
- It is dirty.
- I like reading books.
- He is boring.

- His teaching is boring.
- He was bored in the class.
- I am serious.
- Which is your book?
- Whose book is this?
- Which book?
- Where are my books?
- Where is my bag?
- Here it is.
- Which is your bag?
- Who teaches you English?
- May I join the group?
- You can sit next to me.
- You can sit if you want.
- Do you have a pen?
- Sorry, I don't have pen.
- Don't you have a pen?
- Do you have a spare pen?
- How much is this pen?
- How many pens do you have?
- Give me your pen.
- Give me a choice.
- Can I carry your bags for you?
- Can I leave my bag here?
- Shall I go near the board?
- This classroom has two windows.
- My name doesn't appear on the list.
- Do you like my shoes?
- I cannot open my Tiffin box.

- I am the tallest boy in the class.
- I can run fast and jump up high.
- I want to go down the slide.
- I am going to the library.
- I went to the library to read books.
- I can recommend this book to you.
- It is good. You should try it.
- I have nothing to write.
- I don’t want to study tonight.
- Anand is very good at Maths.
- What do we have to do now?
- What is the meaning of this?
- Could I ask you something?
- Yes, of course you can.
- Do you have the notes from last week class?
- Do we have to write this down?
- What page are we on?
- Do we have to hand in this exercise?
- What do you mean?
- I hate to write test.
- I am sorry, I didn’t hear.
- I promise.
- I didn’t say that, Sir.
- It is 10:15.
- It is time for break.
- What to eat now?
- Let’s have some snacks.
- Who ate my snacks?
- What snacks do you have?

- I used to drink juice.
- For snacks, I eat fruit or nuts.
- I still eat.
- Let's do it!
- That's the end of break. It is 10:25.
- Don't you have homework?
- I don't have homework.
- What is the homework?
- I have a lot of homework to do.
- Show me your homework diary.
- She does her homework.
- I do my homework in the morning.
- I always do my homework after school.
- I have finished the homework.
- I am too lazy to do my homework.
- I could not do my homework because I am sick.
- I will do your homework for you.
- I need to finish this today.
- Thank you for helping me with my homework.
- Do we have to hand in this exercise?
- Could you step aside, please? I can't see the board.
- Can we pack our things now?
- Can I switch on the light?
- Can I switch off the light?
- You know children's day is next Tuesday.
- Shall I open the window?
- Shall I go out?
- Can I sharpen my pencil?
- Could you help me please?

- Shall I come and study with you?
- I learn Hindi.
- How long have you been learning?
- I study English every day.
- Sir, can you explain again?
- Shall I answer the question?
- Can I do the exercise on the board?
- Can you help me study for my exam?
- Could you give us an example of this?
- Can you use this word in a sentence?
- Sir, can you help me, please?
- Tell Vimala, to meet me in the library.
- She may begin her lessons.
- Madam, May I use this computer?
- Can you lend me your textbook?
- May I go near the board?
- May I ask a question?
- I don't know how to describe it.
- Could you help me, please?
- How is this word pronounced?
- What does this mean?
- What does that mean in our language?
- How do you say it in English?
- How do you spell this word?
- How do you pronounce this word?
- I understand now.
- We lost by two marks.
- I failed by one mark.
- I missed a few classes.

- The bell rings at 12:30.
- It is 12:30 lunchtime.
- I am hungry.
- I am going to take lunch.
- I eat lunch with my friends.
- Don't you want to eat lunch?
- What have you got for lunch, Ananya?
- I have sambar rice and a packet of chips.
- He has eaten my chips.
- What time do you have dinner?
- I have dinner at 8 p.m.
- What happened?
- They let me off with just a warning.
- He is late.
- He hasn't come yet.
- Wait for us.
- Don't go. Wait for me.
- Don't talk here. Be quiet.
- I have homework.
- My favorite subject is Maths.
- When do you go to Maths class?
- I have Maths class on Wednesday.
- I go to Maths class at 7 p.m.
- I am going to play. Can you join me?
- How about playing Chess?
- I do not want to play Chess.
- I don't want to play. I have to study.
- Please tell me where to go.
- Sofia goes in.

- Maya goes to fetch water.
- She fell down.
- She got up.
- Mala starts crying.
- She wipes her tears away.
- Nancy borrows the book.
- He stands beside me.
- He stands behind Ajay.
- Where are the boys?
- Over there.
- He is present / absent.
- He has given leave letter, sir.
- He complains too much.
- I didn't hear what you said.
- I didn't catch the sentence.
- They are fighting.
- They often fight.
- You are always talking.
- You are talking too much.
- I will complain you.
- They hit each other.
- She banged her head.
- He pushed me down.
- Please describe what occurred there.
- I cannot remember.
- He admitted that he stole the money.
- I made a mistake.
- It was my mistake.
- Totally my fault!

- He admitted his mistakes.
- I am sorry for what happened.
- I admit my mistake.
- The teacher advised us.
- Excuse me, do you mind if I sit down here?
- Do you have an extra pen I could borrow?
- I forgot to bring my geometry box today.
- If I were you, I would answer the question.
- If I were you, I would have explained in detail.
- It's none of your business, don't ask questions.
- Could you please leave me alone for a while?
- I am looking for someone to help me study.
- Sir, I want to get more marks. What do I have to do?
- I want to improve my English. What do I have to do?
- I will return it as soon as the class is over.
- Read slowly please.
- Madam, I have a question.
- Madam, I have a doubt about this.
- I have done this.
- He and I did this.
- It is easy.
- It is difficult.
- It is different.
- I must study hard.
- I have a lesson in fifteen minutes.
- I prefer studying late night with pin drop silence.
- John, what is in the bag?
- It is English book.
- Is it your notebook?

- The syllabus seems pretty long.
- Please move a bit, I can't see the board.
- Can you play the CD again, please?
- Can I borrow your pen, please?
- After lunch, we will have class.
- It is Maths, Today.
- When is the exam?
- The exam is on next week.
- I have an exam tomorrow.
- I memorized five chapters.
- I studied two lessons.
- I studied five questions.
- It was all I could study.
- I have to study for the exam.
- I still don't understand this.
- When is the homework due?
- What does this word mean?
- How do you say it in English?
- I know nothing.
- I do as you say.
- What a fool!
- What a shame! I failed the test again.
- Talk to me, please.
- Madam, what can I do next?
- Let's do it after school.
- Come and sit here, please.
- Where is Nitya?
- Where is she?
- She is in class.

- Where is Anand?
- He has gone down.
- He is at home.
- Is he sick or something?
- May I clean the board, please?
- Would you lend me a pencil, please?
- Shall I rub the board?
- I couldn't complete my assignment.
- I have got my hands full. Four assignments are due this Friday.
- What subject are they?
- One for Maths, one for Science, and one for English.
- How much time are you given to complete them?
- How can you manage?
- I am afraid that I can't finish.
- I will have to hand them in late.
- Why was that?
- Are you interested in Astronomy?
- Yes I am!
- I read about it every day.
- I am doing it for my love of science.
- Do you like what you study?
- What was it about?
- It was a topic about food.
- What subjects do we have today?
- Physics, Biology and English.
- She helps me with my science homework.
- Why aren't you preparing for the test?
- I have everything memorized.
- Do you feel nervous?

- I always feel nervous before the exam.
- Try your best, my friend.
- We will study together.
- I have trouble concentrating too.
- My last score was not good.
- I am confident this time.
- Review your lesson carefully.
- Some exercises are very difficult.
- How did your science exam go?
- The results didn't turn out to be good.
- I passed with flying colours!
- How was your result for the science test?
- Not bad, I got 50.
- Maths is really hard for me.
- I always confused with formulas.
- Excuse me sir I need mark.
- There might be an error in my test paper.
- I think that the total is incorrect.
- I checked well.
- Let's double-check the answers to be sure.
- I do not see any mistakes.
- I am going to take a second look.
- Let's total it.
- I will try to get good mark.
- This one right here should be right.
- I missed a few classes.
- I come to school regularly.
- Sometimes I become absent-minded.
- I was over the moon when I finally passed my exam.

- Algebra is very confusing.
- She got a scholarship.
- I am going to physics laboratory.
- How many girls are there?
- There are seven girls in the class.
- The teacher was absent from the class.
- My teacher is very strict.
- He is strict but also has a special teaching style.
- My teacher is a laid-back.
- She is so laid-back.
- Nothing worried him, he was really laid back.
- She is always the centre of attention.
- I learned a lot of new things.
- My teacher is one of the best teachers that I have ever had.
- He is very knowledgeable and funny.
- Every student likes the English teacher.
- Can I join your class?
- He always tells a joke to begin a lesson.
- Ms. Sheela is good, but she is boring sometimes.
- She is a good teacher.
- She spoke to me in English and I replied in English.
- How do I fill out this form?
- He gave us some general instruction.
- I am going home now. See you tomorrow.
- I am going outside/inside.
- He and I are classmates.
- He may be late.
- I arrived here early.
- I was absent yesterday.

- I can’t come next week.
- I went for a family wedding.
- I attended my sister’s marriage.
- Sorry, for being late madam.
- Next week, we will have a competition at school.
- We are in the same class.
- They are not making noise in the class.
- Where have you kept the practical note?
- Where do you keep your note?
- I kept my note here.
- Hey. What is going on?
- Have you seen my note?
- Have you seen my stapler?
- No, I haven’t.
- How is it going at school?
- Give me time to finish this.
- I forgot about the project and the deadline is tomorrow.
- What are you going to do?
- I don’t know what to do.
- At what time do you usually get up in the morning?
- At what time do you usually go to school?
- When does the school van arrive?
- When does the exam start?
- When does the school open?
- When is your class?
- When do they come to school?
- When is the lunchtime?
- I ran to get my bag.
- He is good at singing.

- He will study on Friday.
- Have you got a friend?
- Your friend is very selfish.
- Give him some advice.
- Do you worry about failing exams?
- No, I am not worry about it.
- Do your parents complain about writing homework too much?
- Do your parents complain about playing too much?
- How often do you complain about doing a lot of homework?
- Do you dislike studying?
- My favourite subjects are Maths, Science and English.
- Where have you been?
- I have been at the canteen
- Does your school have a canteen?
- Do you eat in the school canteen?
- Every day I enjoy my lunch in the school canteen.
- They finish classes at three o'clock.
- I was very bored in the science lesson. I almost fell asleep.
- Are you joining the contest?
- I will not participate in this competition.
- I was in the library.
- I have to prepare for the exam.
- That is out of the question.
- We have to get results.
- He bought two copies of book.
- Where did you put my book?
- The teacher scolded the students for no reason.
- Do you prefer playing or watching sports?
- How many hours of sports do you have in school?

- How often do you play?
- Have you ever won a medal in a sports competition?
- When is the sports day?
- Where is it going to be held?
- I play games with my friends in the playground.
- Can I play with you?
- We will not play with you.
- I am sorry for everything.
- I am out of practice.
- We are going to practice.
- Have you seen Vanitha?
- May I join the group?
- Now go practice.
- He practiced everyday at school.
- Madam, my bag has gone.
- Are you walking home?
- We go to school together.
- I am sorry. I couldn’t return the book yesterday.
- I must return this book today.
- Thank you for correcting this mistake.
- What ails you?
- Do you feel better now?
- I am unwell.
- I am bleeding.
- I feel feverish.
- I have a pain in my left shoulder.
- I feel sick.
- My stomach is upset.
- Do you have any allergies?

- I am allergic to dust.
- My nose is running.
- I have a fever.
- I feel sick.
- I have a cold.
- I hurt my leg when I run.
- I sprained my ankle.
- I cry because I am in pain.
- I have a severe headache.
- I will dress the wound.
- I will put the plaster.
- Don't worry there is no serious problem.
- What happen?
- I got sick, and so I couldn't come to school.
- I can't come because I got fever.
- I am very sorry I lied.
- I am very ashamed of myself.
- Everyone laughed at her reply.
- Don't do such things.
- I admitted that I didn't do that.
- You will pay for your mischief.
- I had fun on the slide.
- Can I answer the question?
- Can we pack our things now?
- The weather is pleasant.
- It is about to rain.
- Look over there. It is raining.
- It is drizzling.
- It is raining heavily outside.

- I play with my friends in the evening.
- I will see him on his birthday.
- How do you come to school every day?
- I came by bus.
- I came on foot.
- I walk. My house is near my school.
- I come to school by walk.
- I go to school on foot.
- She always goes to school on foot.
- My legs always get tired.
- I came with my father by bike.
- Who will come and pick you up?
- My father will come and pick me up at 4 o'clock.
- I usually walk to school but my dad drove me today.
- I ride my bicycle to school every day.
- Has the bell rung?
- It is time to go home.
- It is 3:30, the end of the school.
- See you at school tomorrow.
- See you on Monday.
- See you this evening.
- Good morning, teacher.
- May I sit down?
- May I ask a question?
- Could you please repeat that?
- I did not understand the lesson.
- Can you explain it again?
- May I go to the washroom?
- I have completed my homework.

- I forgot my notebook at home.
- Please check my assignment.
- I have a doubt in this chapter.
- Could you help me with this problem?
- I was absent yesterday.
- What is today's homework?
- May I answer the question?
- I need more time to finish.
- Thank you for teaching us.
- Sorry for being late.
- I could not complete the work.
- May I borrow a book from the library?
- Could you speak slowly, please?
- I am unable to understand this topic.
- Can you give another example?
- I will try my best.
- I do not understand.
- Please repeat.
- Can you explain?
- I know the answer.
- I do not know.
- I have a question.
- May I come in?
- May I go out?
- May I drink water?
- May I use the washroom?
- I am late.
- I am sorry for being late.
- I forgot my notebook.

- I forgot my homework.
- I completed my homework.
- Please check my work.
- I have submitted my project.
- Could you guide me?
- I appreciate your help.
- Please correct my mistakes.
- Can you explain the instructions?
- I am interested in this topic.
- May I write on the board?
- Could you please check my notebook?
- I need help with pronunciation.
- Thank you for your support.
- I am trying to improve.
- May I leave early today?
- I did not hear the announcement.
- Could you tell me the exam date?
- I have a medical appointment tomorrow.
- Please excuse my absence.
- I respect your advice.
- I enjoyed today's lesson.
- Could you recommend a good book?
- I want to improve my English speaking.
- Can you explain the grammar rule?
- I am confused about this question.
- May I participate in the competition?
- Thank you for encouraging us.
- I appreciate your feedback.
- I need extra practice in mathematics.

- Could you help me after class?
- I forgot to bring my textbook.
- I will submit it tomorrow.
- Please give me one more chance.
- I am preparing for the exam.
- Can you suggest study tips?
- I could not attend the class due to illness.
- Thank you for understanding.
- Could you explain the project requirements?
- I need clarification on this topic.
- May I work with my partner?
- I am interested in joining the club.
- Please allow me to answer.
- I am sorry for disturbing the class.
- I will not repeat this mistake.
- Could you evaluate my presentation?
- Thank you for your valuable guidance.
- I learned a lot from today's class.
- Could you share additional notes?
- I need help with my assignment.
- May I submit my work tomorrow?
- I am finding this lesson difficult.
- Could you provide more exercises?
- I want to improve my confidence.
- Thank you for motivating us.
- I would like to participate in the debate.
- Could you explain the experiment once more?
- I appreciate your patience.
- I have practiced the speech.

- May I present my project now?
- I am grateful for your advice.
- Could you please review my answers?
- I will work harder next time.
- Please help me improve my writing skills.
- I am eager to learn more.
- Could you explain the meaning of this word?
- I would like to clarify my doubt.
- Thank you for giving us this opportunity.
- I understand the lesson now.
- Could you provide some homework examples?
- I need permission to leave early.
- I am ready for the presentation.
- Please guide me for the competition.
- I respect your teaching methods.
- Thank you for inspiring us.
- I will complete the task on time.
- I appreciate your encouragement.
- Have a nice day, teacher.

FOR ***TEACHERS***

- Please come in.
- Get in.
- Listen!
- Speak!
- Read!
- Write!
- Good morning, everybody.
- Be quiet, please.

- Come here, please.
- Stand up, please.
- Sit down, please.
- Get down.
- Get out
- Get last.
- Go out.
- Go ahead.
- Come over, here.
- Follow me.
- Lead me.
- Sit beside him.
- Stop talking and be quiet.
- Sit aside.
- Sit here.
- Step aside.
- Set aside.
- No excuse.
- Move please.
- Move aside.
- Move a bit.
- Nobody move.
- Stop doing it.
- Silence, please.
- Keep quiet.
- Don’t run here.
- Don’t run fast.
- Go slow.
- Go along.

- Go home.
- Go left.
- Go to class.
- Go for a walk.
- Come soon.
- Clear the way.
- Make a space.
- Make way.
- Start writing.
- Stop writing.
- Take down.
- Note it down.
- Recall it.
- Try to say.
- Stand back.
- Stay together.
- Gather here.
- Get together.
- Stand still.
- Sit still.
- Stay where you are.
- Call him in.
- Sit up straight please.
- Stop chatting.
- Stop talking.
- Stop doing that.
- Shut your eyes.
- Take your seat.
- Put kneel down.

- Put down.
- Be on time for class.
- Please speak slower.
- Now, settle down.
- Show me your nails.
- Cut your nails.
- Your hair looks unkempt.
- Comb your hair.
- Get your haircut tomorrow.
- Button up your shirt.
- Tuck in your shirt.
- Button your shirt.
- Don’t pop your collar.
- Your shirt is dirty.
- Remove your shirt.
- Pay attention!
- Allow me to speak.
- Do what I tell you.
- Do as I say.
- Take your note.
- Write down.
- Write it in pencil.
- Everybody is focused.
- No one can leave.
- What happened?
- What do you want?
- Don’t run in the classroom.
- Get out of here.
- You may go.

- Mend your ways.
- Sita, please come here.
- Can you come here?
- Get back to your seat.
- Leave the place.
- Please, be careful.
- Be quiet.
- Be ready.
- Be calm.
- Go to your room.
- Get your things.
- Pack your bags.
- Pack your things.
- Here's your key.
- Pick up a book.
- Take your book.
- Open your book.
- Close your book.
- Read your book.
- Step in closer.
- Avoid mistakes.
- Avoid overwriting.
- Learn good manners.
- Form a queue.
- Go stand on the corner.
- Go and drink some water.
- Please get some water.
- Be silent in the library.
- Watch and learn.

- Nobody listen.
- Let’s take a break.
- Let him in.
- Let me out.
- Let him try.
- Let it be.
- Let me think.
- Let him sleep.
- Let me see how good you are.
- Let’s get back to the class.
- Let you go.
- Let me know.
- Let’s see what they have.
- Let her go.
- Let’s go.
- Let’s help him.
- Let me read.
- Let me speak.
- Please write it down.
- Stop me if you have any doubt.
- Take out your notebook.
- Take it outside.
- Please stand quietly.
- Please stand in a line.
- I will go after you.
- You can ask me.
- It is time to begin.
- Calm down now.
- Please stop talking.

- Stop whispering.
- Can you stop talking?
- Can you do it again?
- Will you shut up?
- Stop playing inside.
- Stop crying.
- Keep your books neat.
- Come and sit down here.
- Did you go to kindergarten?
- Write the lesson.
- Memorize the poem.
- Learn by heart.
- Give me a chalk piece.
- Get me a duster.
- Erase the board, please.
- Rub the board.
- Clean the board.
- Shall I rub the board?
- Would you clean the board?
- Just clean this part.
- Rub everything off.
- Do you get it?
- Do exercise 7.
- Try exercise 8.
- Look over here.
- Look at me.
- Listen here.
- Listen up.
- What is this?

- This is an apple.
- What is that?
- That is an apple.
- What are these?
- These are apples.
- What are those?
- Those are apples.
- Focus on the lesson.
- Focus on your studies.
- Read this chapter.
- Write the answer.
- Draw the next diagram.
- Take it up.
- Try it.
- Jump to the 12th page.
- Okay carry on.
- Not too bad.
- Not so well.
- Respect others.
- Sit up straight everybody.
- Don’t lean over your desk.
- I am your English teacher.
- I will teach you English.
- Take your seats.
- Introduce yourself.
- Say your name.
- Spell your name.
- Please sit down.
- Take your book.

- Are you going to read?
- Is everybody ready to start?
- I don't start until everyone is quiet.
- How many of you are without books?
- Shall I read slowly?
- Read slowly.
- Read aloud.
- More loudly.
- Say loudly.
- Read one by one.
- I will repeat that.
- Good let's give him a hand.
- Take a look at this.
- Take page 10.
- Stand up and read.
- Bring your book over here.
- I am talking to you.
- Do you hear me?
- Come over here.
- Please read.
- Speak out.
- Now hear this.
- Read the paragraph.
- You should read a lot.
- Tie your shoelace.
- Pack your things.
- Roll up your sleeves.
- Put the books in order.
- Put it over there.

- That is their book.
- Is this pen yours?
- Dust the table.
- Clean the table.
- Clean the cobweb.
- Tidy up your classroom.
- Clean your room.
- Put the things in the box.
- Light the candle.
- Close the tap.
- Turn on.
- Turn off the lights.
- Switch on the fan.
- Put the fan on high speed.
- Put the thing in the cupboard.
- Water the plant.
- Form two lines.
- Let's go downstairs.
- Quicken your step.
- Pick up the toys.
- Go and play with your friends.
- Did you lock the door?
- Go and take some rest.
- Keep everything ready.
- Obey my order.
- Do as I say.
- Do the homework.
- Go, I will come to the class.
- Wash your hands.

- Watch your head.
- Watch your step.
- They are in the class.
- Boys go to play.
- Girls go to the library.
- I allow him as class leader.
- The book is on the table.
- Your book is in the cupboard.
- Take the chair.
- Please take a chair.
- Go and get a chair.
- The chair is beside the table.
- Put the chair in this way.
- Come on everybody. It's time to eat.
- Are you ready to go to library?
- Hand me your books.
- I need to return these books.
- Shut up your mouth.
- Hold your tongue.
- She recited a poem.
- You are a good boy.
- Be a good girl.
- Behave yourself.
- Act like a lady.
- Act like a gentleman.
- Stop it.
- Don't touch that.
- Don't touch it.
- Put that down.

- Put that away.
- Stop teasing others.
- Make friends.
- Leave him alone.
- Meet your class teacher.
- How many times have I told you?
- Don't make me tell you again.
- Reply to my question.
- Will you shut up?
- Repeat the instruction, please.
- What happen to your face?
- What do they study?
- They are studying science.
- Is everyone's diary signed?
- Who signs your diary at home?
- Read this page five times at home.
- Look straight ahead.
- Look to the left.
- Look to the right.
- Join your hands and close your eyes.
- Take pledge.
- Slow down, please.
- Go slowly, please.
- Go forward.
- Look behind you.
- Could you not speak so fast?
- Can everyone tidy up now, please?
- Put things in order now, please.
- Arrange the books in order.

- You should not move from your position.
- Why is your uniform dirty?
- I have told you many times to keep your room tidy.
- Do you know English?
- Get me the register.
- Who can clean the board?
- Where are you taking this?
- I am your Maths teacher.
- I will be teaching you Maths.
- I am going to take attendance.
- Now let me call the roll.
- Attend your roll call.
- I will call your names.
- How do you spell your name?
- Who is not here today?
- No one is absent.
- Let's see who is absent.
- Why is he on leave today?
- Who is absent today?
- Is anybody absent today?
- Who is missing?
- Why is he absent?
- Is he sick?
- Is she feeling sick?
- Can you explain why you were late?
- Why were you absent yesterday?
- Why don't you reply to my question?
- Why do you tell a lie to me?
- Are you making excuses again?

- Why are you late?
- I have been looking for you.
- I haven't seen you for a longtime.
- Where have you been?
- What is the reason for coming late?
- Are they late?
- Why are you late?
- Don't be late next time.
- He is always late.
- You are too late.
- You are late by ten minutes.
- You are late again.
- Don't be late.
- Be punctual.
- He is never late.
- Is he coming to the school regularly?
- You should not sleep late.
- How many girls are there in your class?
- There are seven girls in the class.
- What is the name of that girl?
- Where have you been?
- Try to be on time.
- How is your fever?
- When is Sita coming?
- Now settle down.
- Hear my words.
- Can you hear me?
- Do you get it?
- Don't you see?

- Stop it now.
- Let's stop now.
- Is your test over?
- Is your house far away?
- Is this your pen?
- I need a pencil.
- I need a piece of paper.
- I need a book.
- Let me see.
- Would you move your desk back?
- Who told you that?
- Who is your class leader?
- Who is your class teacher?
- Let me think about it.
- What do you see?
- Look at the picture. What is it?
- Raise your hands.
- Put up your hands.
- Put down your hands.
- Put your hands down.
- We'll start now, if you don't mind.
- Can you open your science book?
- Do you all have your English book?
- This lesson is important. Please focus.
- Let us discuss first.
- Shall we come into the story?
- Let's read the paragraph together.
- Can I have your attention, please?
- Wait I am repeating.

- Repeat after me.
- Please read more slowly.
- Please speak slowly.
- Listen to me, please.
- Are you ready to listen?
- Can everybody hear?
- Listen to my pronunciation.
- May I have your attention, please?
- Please, pay attention to Sam.
- He is reading.
- Shall I begin?
- Is it clear to you?
- Do you follow me?
- Do you understand?
- Where were we?
- Do you remember where we were?
- Where did we stop last time?
- Do you read?
- Who wants to read?
- Have you got a book?
- What page are we on?
- I am ready. May I start it?
- Listen and repeat.
- Listen and watch carefully.
- Now listen and repeat after me.
- Am I loud?
- Am I audible?
- Am I too fast?
- Am I right?

- Don't stop middle of the sentence.
- Read loudly and clearly.
- Start now.
- Did you understand what I said?
- Am I talking too fast?
- Do you know what I mean?
- Do you know what I am talking about?
- We are going to learn something new today.
- We are going to learn trigonometry today.
- Let's move on to the next page.
- Turn to the next page.
- Turn the page.
- Open your books on page 9, please.
- Open your books to page ten.
- Do the exercise on page 8.
- Turn to page 45.
- Share a book.
- Please turn to number 12 in your book.
- Was that too difficult for you to read?
- Who is next?
- It is your turn now.
- Let me explain.
- He will explain.
- Please explain it.
- Can you explain why?
- Does anyone know what this is?
- Can you guess what it is?
- Almost right.
- I will teach you.

- I will explain it later.
- Listen and I will explain.
- Don't ask me to explain.
- I cannot explain everything.
- I don't have time to explain.
- What does this mean?
- Can you explain this to me?
- I have already explained that poem.
- Let us see who can answer this question.
- Can you answer this question?
- Feel free to ask me any questions about this lesson.
- Who is going to answer this question?
- What do you know about this story?
- What did you learn about this story?
- Can someone explain this to me?
- Would you explain what this is?
- Can you describe it?
- Can you describe the picture?
- Raise your hands to speak.
- Raise your hand if you know the answer.
- Don't shout raise your hands if you know the answer
- Kamal, answer this question.
- Vimal, can you answer this questions?
- Answer the question.
- Do you know the answer?
- Does anyone know the answer?
- No one can tell the answer.
- What is the answer?
- Did you prepare well?

- Can you tell me the answer?
- Does anyone know the answer?
- What does this mean?
- Did you understand this lesson?
- How do you say it in French?
- No one knows the answer.
- Please speak up. I can't hear you.
- Could you speak up? We can't hear you very well.
- To every question, he responded 'I don't know'.
- Vimal stand up and tell.
- It's better than nothing.
- Give examples for Noun.
- Do you understand what I mean?
- What do you think it says?
- It is important that you understand.
- I am glad that you understand.
- Can we do it another time?
- I want to do something useful.
- Could you hand that to me?
- It was pretty easy to do that.
- That wasn't easy to translate.
- I won't tell you this again.
- Are you familiar with this?
- Watch me do it again.
- We should finish this exercise next day.
- We have completed this chapter.
- We will continue this lesson on next Monday.
- You should never leave anything unfinished.
- I think that won't be easy to do.

- I think you can get it.
- Are you prepared to do this?
- You already know what to do.
- You should do that by yourself.
- You must do it yourself.
- Why don't we do it right now?
- It is nice, who did this?
- I want to know how you did it.
- Do this.
- And then do this.
- Please tell me what this is.
- Do you have an explanation?
- Wait, your turn Anand.
- That's all for now. We will see next class.
- That's all for today. You can go now.
- Do you enjoy studying English?
- How long are you studying this?
- Do they talk English?
- What can I do to help you?
- You are always procrastinating.
- The sooner you learn better.
- I am glad you have learnt your lesson.
- You are a good student humble and respectful.
- He could have studied well but he was too lazy.
- I am doing it for your own good.
- Give me a different solution.
- I have never heard of it before.
- No whispering, please.
- No noise, please.

- I have told you repeatedly. You don't listen!
- I want pin drop silence in the class.
- I want pin drop silence, not even the sound of your breath.
- Make your own story.
- You made mistake.
- Let's go on to question number 3.
- Check your answers on page 10.
- Take out your pen.
- I will give you ten minutes.
- Lesson 4 is easy.
- Choose between these two.
- Check the answers.
- Have you checked the answer?
- Take your note and write.
- Pick up the pen.
- Now mark the important questions.
- I have no choice.
- That's all.
- Why are you talking?
- Put down the pen.
- Copy it.
- Copy this in your notebook.
- Go back to your place.
- Sit back to back.
- Stop making such a noise.
- Write on the board.
- Look at the black board.
- Come to the board, please.
- Come here to the front.

- Come up here.
- Face the board.
- Please take down.
- What are you talking about?
- What do you want to become?
- Write it down here, please.
- Please write it here.
- Can you write your name of this list?
- You are taking too long.
- Are you following me?
- Carry on this exercise, I will be back in a moment.
- Keep quiet, I will be back in five minutes.
- Would you mind the class till I am back?
- You don't have to shout. I can hear you clearly.
- I want you to do a project about……
- Do this by yourself with the help of internet?
- Learn your lesson and do your homework.
- This is your homework for today.
- There is no homework today.
- Where is your homework assignment, John?
- Show me your homework.
- Did you finish your homework?
- Did you complete the homework?
- Did you complete your homework?
- Have you finished your homework?
- Have you completed the homework?
- Can you show me your notebook?
- You should finish your homework.
- You should have finished this homework.

- Why didn't you finish it?
- I want you to do that at home.
- Are you doing the last sum?
- Do you need help with this sum?
- Do the first exercise.
- Complete this immediately.
- What did you do on the weekend?
- What are you doing?
- How do you get that?
- What do you want?
- They are having fun.
- It is not bad.
- It is good.
- It is near here.
- This is what I wanted.
- What day is today?
- What date is today?
- Tell me. What am I teaching now?
- Why is he dull?
- He has a cold so he is very tired.
- You look awful. Lie down and have a rest.
- Where is John?
- You simply waste your time.
- You stay there.
- You may go now.
- Go back to your seat.
- I know her from school.
- She doesn't listen to me.
- You have to mend your ways.

- Earn good name.
- In which class are you studying?
- You must not be absent without leave letter.
- Don't let it happen again.
- You need to get to a hospital.
- What do you have for your breakfast?
- Write what I say.
- Do what I say.
- Whose mistake is it?
- Whose handwriting is this?
- Correct the mistakes.
- Work on your own.
- Please, work in pairs.
- Ask your partner.
- Get into group of three.
- There are too many in this group.
- I will divide you into two teams.
- There are four of us.
- The students stood in a circle.
- Vimala is the first to finish all.
- Where are Ramu and Somu going?
- Do you prefer studying alone or with your friends?
- Put away your books.
- Where is the book?
- It's over there.
- What shape is it?
- It is a triangle.
- What shape are they?
- They are square.

- What shapes are they?
- They are triangle.
- What do you see?
- I see two rectangles.
- What colour are they?
- They are red.
- How many squares do you see?
- Be ready for tomorrow's test on Algebra.
- Hurry up, get ready for the test.
- Are you ready to write a test?
- Close your books.
- Put away.
- Put your things away.
- May I sharpen my pencil?
- May I borrow a pen?
- Are you ready for the mid-term test?
- Everybody take a piece of paper.
- Take out a piece of paper.
- Can you pass the paper?
- Pass this to the back.
- Help each other.
- Pass the paper.
- Hand in your test paper.
- Finish it soon.
- You won't finish on time.
- You are not writing fast.
- I want you to finish it quickly.
- You have five minutes.
- Have you all finished?

- There's the bell. It is time to stop.
- You still have five minutes to go.
- It's time to finish.
- It is time to stop.
- Time's up.
- Time's up. Put your pen down and pass your test paper.
- First tie your paper and then write.
- No more time finish it quickly.
- I can't remember.
- Write fast.
- Stop now.
- Thread, please.
- Tie your paper.
- There is a pin drop silence in the examination hall.
- How did you write the test?
- Did you write well?
- Yes, I wrote well.
- It was easy.
- It was difficult.
- It's a difficult question.
- It was tough.
- Let me check.
- Let's see how well you perform.
- The result will be announced tomorrow.
- Everyone was silent when the teacher announces the results.
- She failed to appear in the exam.
- Have you all got your marks?
- Have you checked the paper?
- How much have you got, Rahul?

- Are there many failures in Maths?
- How much have you got in Science?
- Is it enough?
- You have to improve a lot.
- You have to pass the test.
- I passed the test.
- His performance was not very good.
- Did you show marks to your parents?
- You must try your best to pass the exam.
- Gather the papers and bring them here.
- Can you gather all of the papers together?
- Is it true?
- I know what I said.
- I will grant you.
- Let's try again.
- Don't worry nobody is perfect first time.
- Your friends are spoiling you.
- Let's practice English.
- Be careful or you will fall down.
- Do you have school tomorrow?
- Did you bring your lunch?
- Did you return the book?
- If you borrow it, bring it back.
- When are you going to complete the practical note?
- Who teaches you English grammar?
- When will you come?
- When is the library closed?
- When are your exams starting?
- Why are you laughing?

- Write five times.
- Throw it out.
- Clear off your desk.
- Watch out! Are you all right?
- How many people go to the excursion?
- How do you say that in English?
- Can you spell TEACHER, please?
- How do you spell this word?
- How do you spell 'ETYMOLOGY'?
- What does it mean in English?
- Translate it, please.
- Clean the board, please.
- Come to the blackboard, please.
- Look at your map.
- Look at the picture.
- Draw a picture.
- What is in the picture?
- What do you know about the picture?
- Tell me about the picture.
- Keep your eyes open.
- Form a line.
- What is this in English?
- I don't know what it is.
- Go and ask for help.
- Don't help him.
- No one knows.
- If you have any doubts ask me.
- Feel free to ask.
- It is time to finish the exercise.

- Label the picture.
- Unscramble the words.
- Put the sentence in order.
- Underline the sentence.
- Cross out the word.
- Circle the word.
- Match the items.
- Fill out this form, please.
- Write your name here, please.
- Write down your name and the date on a piece of paper.
- Sign at the bottom of the paper.
- Give it to me.
- I will meet you after work.
- What book you want?
- You need to be very quiet.
- You need to be absolutely silent.
- Your performance was very bad. You need to improve.
- If you want to pass your exams, keep studying.
- Their performance was awful.
- I am happy for your achievement.
- I am happy and excited.
- Is anyone in your class going to the Exhibition?
- I don’t want anyone to miss this.
- It is very important that you listen carefully.
- It is essential that you listen carefully.
- It is very important that you do exactly what I say.
- I want the classroom to be very clean.
- I want the room to be spotless.
- He is a very good student.

- Keep your work neat and organized.
- You have never missed an assignment.
- One person talk at a time.
- Write your address.
- Why did you go there?
- Why did you go out?
- Did you ask permission?
- Write a letter.
- Who did this?
- I didn't.
- I am.
- I don't remember his name.
- Are you kidding me?
- Are you sure, you did that?
- Listen carefully, please.
- Observe carefully.
- Have you seen it?
- May be you should go home and get some rest.
- You should report it to your class teacher.
- Why are you shouting like this?
- I asked you not to go there. Did you listen to me?
- Work quietly. Don't disturb others who are studying or writing.
- He is a very good player.
- Play well.
- Let's start the competition.
- Did you win the competition?
- What time do you get up in the morning?
- Form a line and wait for the bell.
- Did you get the note?

- He is absolutely a terrific player.
- Your English is good.
- His English is superb.
- The ground is dry.
- He is a naughty little boy.
- Don't mind it.
- Your words are meaningful.
- Do you have a computer at home?
- Do you have internet connection?
- Do you come to school by bus?
- Maria, go to the map and find Australia.
- Tell me who discovered America?
- Tell me what you remember.
- Will you show me the picture?
- What are you talking about?
- What have you done?
- You are hovering around here. What do you want?
- Has she gone?
- Ask her to come here.
- This is your handwriting, isn't it?
- What is happening?
- Is everything ok?
- Are you sure about that?
- Why are you fighting?
- Why did you beat him?
- You never listen to me.
- What is wrong with you?
- What is going on in here?
- What is going on there? Stop talking.

- What is going on in the last bench?
- What happen to you two?
- What is going on with you two?
- Don’t you two ever stop fighting?
- What are you trying to say?
- What? How is this possible?
- Is there a problem?
- Tell me, what it is?
- He is a mischievous boy.
- He is innocent.
- I have faith in you.
- I am sure he is guilty.
- Why did you hit him?
- You take him to the hospital.
- He gives more trouble in the class.
- Your son is making trouble.
- This is the limit.
- Keep your promise.
- I am unable to bear his trouble.
- I can't bear his trouble.
- Let me know.
- You go and bring him
- Ask him to come here.
- You ask him to come here.
- You bring him here.
- Don't tell this.
- What is the excuse this time?
- You should be punished for doing this.
- You should be ashamed of yourself.

- Jack was stunned.
- I heard the news through him.
- How dare you talk to me like this?
- Were you out of your mind to do such a thing?
- Do you think you are very smart?
- Do you think I am not aware of it?
- You are always complaining about something.
- Behave yourself otherwise, I will send you out.
- How dare you hit me?
- Why did you do that?
- What did you say?
- What did you do?
- I know nothing in this connection.
- That cannot be true.
- You ask question to yourself.
- Have you ever lied to a teacher?
- Come on you two.
- I have told you repeatedly, do not shout in the class.
- Why do you keep making the same mistakes repeatedly?
- Don't turn your back.
- I asked the students to be frank with me.
- I just want you to be straight with me.
- I don't believe you anyway.
- Don't let small problems upset you.
- Don't talk to me like that.
- I don't want your sympathy.
- Nobody wants you to do this.
- I didn't mean to hurt you.
- The problem is you.

- Come on you two.
- You two stay here.
- You two may leave.
- I know about you two.
- It is no use separating them.
- He never listens.
- John always troubled others.
- Why are you talking?
- What are you talking?
- Did I ask you?
- Did you push him down?
- Who made this mess?
- How did you break this?
- Do you know who it is?
- You should do what I suggest.
- Do you want to say something?
- It appears to me you are mistaken.
- It appears to me that he was wrong.
- I want to know why you are here.
- I know what you mean.
- I know what you are thinking.
- Do you know anything about this?
- I have found it.
- You are putting words in my mouth.
- Stop putting words in my mouth.
- You cannot fool me.
- That is not fair.
- There is always a solution to any problem.
- That's what I told.

- Save yourself from the trouble.
- I told you to be careful.
- I know you shouldn't do that.
- You do not have to answer that.
- I do not want to compromise.
- It is a very serious allegation.
- That doesn't work for me.
- Come here, both of you.
- You are not a student.
- I think this is a big mistake.
- I have nothing more to say.
- Stop harassing me.
- Please don't lie to us.
- You are not speaking the truth.
- Why are you crying?
- Tears do not solve any problem.
- It's no use crying.
- Don't pretend.
- Don't be ashamed of yourself.
- Don't talk back to me.
- Just get out of here.
- Get out of my sight.
- Get lost.
- What are you doing here now?
- Everyone knows this.
- It is time to stop doing that.
- What did they say to you?
- Don't tell her about it.
- That's not your problem anymore.

- What is the matter with everybody?
- You should have consulted me first.
- I can’t explain why it happened.
- He mentioned your name to me.
- Do you want to say a few words?
- It is evident that you told a lie.
- I am not going to ask again.
- I have to ask you some questions.
- You don’t like school, do you?
- What is the use of talking?
- How are you going to fix that?
- I have to find out the truth.
- He described exactly what happened.
- We want to know what happened.
- I have some questions for you.
- Keep control.
- Your excuse was very bad.
- His excuse was pathetic.
- I want to know what happens.
- I was unaware of the problem.
- That is why I called you.
- This problem should come to an end.
- We don’t want this to happen again.
- We will forgive you this time.
- Who is coming to see you?
- Does your mother know this?
- Have you informed your parents?
- Ask your parents to come and meet me tomorrow.
- You have to obey your parents.

- When do we meet your parents?
- When do your parents meet us?
- Ask your parents and confirm tomorrow?
- Those who like to come with me, please come.
- Go this way.
- Please make sure that the door is locked.
- I should probably leave tomorrow.
- Up to 30 people can sit in the room.
- Sam is a good student.
- Anand is a good boy.
- She sings really well.
- Nirmala speaks French and English.
- Can you dance?
- In which event are you taking part?
- Where are they?
- What are you doing in here?
- She is dancing.
- When do you practice the piano?
- When is it convenient for you?
- You have to be ready.
- Throw the ball to Arun.
- You need more practice.
- Why are you calling me?
- When are you going to finish?
- We are not ready.
- I don't want to play this game.
- Do you want to take a break?
- I don't have time to exercise.
- He was in good spirits.

- You can go home now.
- You will have to come tomorrow.
- I will take you to the bus stop.
- She behaves well.
- His character is not good.
- I know that you are a good student.
- Better luck next time.
- Ram can write poetry very well.
- Which game do you like to play? Football or Cricket.
- Where is the fire extinguisher?
- Write the date.
- Write the heading.
- Read the lesson.
- Repeat after me.
- Speak loudly.
- Speak slowly.
- Follow the instructions.
- May I drink water?
- May I go to the toilet?
- May I sharpen my pencil?
- May I borrow a pen?
- Can you help me?
- Please explain again.
- Can I answer?
- Work in pairs.
- Work in groups.
- Discuss with your partner.
- Read the question.
- Write the answer.

- Match the words.
- Tick the correct answer.
- Underline the keyword.
- Stay in your seat.
- Raise your hand.
- Wait for your turn.
- Follow the rules.
- Mark your attendance.
- Who is absent today?
- Write the homework.
- Submit your notebook.
- Pack your things.
- Clean your desk.
- Wipe the board.
- Turn on the lights.
- Today we have a test.
- Time is up.
- Check your answers.
- Submit your paper.
- Read the instructions.
- Answer all the questions.
- Don’t leave blanks.
- Keep it up!
- Try again.
- You can do it.
- Excellent answer!
- That was close.
- You are improving.
- I am proud of you.

- Any questions?
- Review the lesson.
- Class is over.
- Pack your bags.
- Line up quietly.
- Read silently.
- Copy from the board.
- Don't erase it.
- Look at the screen.
- Bring your books.
- Sit in your place.
- Take out the worksheet given yesterday.
- Complete the task within ten minutes.
- Write full sentences, not short forms.
- Explain your answer clearly.
- Don't skip any steps.
- Use a ruler for straight lines.
- Highlight the important points.
- Keep your notebooks organized.
- Submit your assignments on time.
- Don't scribble on your books.
- Your handwriting needs improvement.
- You have made a great effort.
- Your explanation is very clear.
- Please check your spellings.
- You need to focus more.
- You are capable of better work.
- Try to participate more in class.
- Your project is well presented.

- You followed the instructions correctly.
- Don't repeat the same mistakes.
- What did you learn today?
- Who wants to answer this?
- What do you think about this topic?
- Do you agree or disagree?
- Why do you think so?
- Can someone give another example?
- Please share your opinion.
- That's an interesting point.
- Let's discuss this as a class.
- Write your thoughts in one paragraph.
- Choose a leader for your group.
- Share your ideas with your team.
- Make sure everyone participates.
- Divide the work equally.
- Present your findings to the class.
- Listen to each other.
- Don't argue unnecessarily.
- Work together patiently.
- Complete the group task.
- Turn on your computer.
- Open the document.
- Save your file.
- Don't change the settings.
- Watch the video carefully.
- Answer the questions on the screen.
- Don't press random keys.
- Charge your device.

- Keep your headphones ready.
- Follow the digital rules.
- Take responsibility for your actions.
- Be respectful to your classmates.
- Be kind to everyone.
- Don't waste your time.
- Don't throw trash on the floor.
- Maintain discipline during activities.
- Avoid unnecessary complaints.
- Report any issues to the teacher.
- Be on time for class.
- Do not use foul language.
- Compare your answer with your partner's.
- Identify the main idea of the passage.
- Summarize the paragraph in your own words.
- Analyze the question before writing.
- Provide reasons for your answer.
- Read the instructions thoroughly.
- Pay attention to the details.
- Rewrite the incorrect sentence.
- Solve it step by step.
- Organize your points logically.
- Let's brainstorm some ideas.
- Who disagrees with this idea?
- What evidence can support this?
- How can we improve this solution?
- Is there any alternative method?
- Think critically before answering.
- This topic requires careful analysis.

- Take notes while listening.
- Use complete sentences in your discussion.
- Speak with confidence.
- What is your doubt?
- Can you repeat the question?
- Please clarify your point.
- That is not the correct answer.
- Let's try it another way.
- Think before you speak.
- Don't interrupt others.
- I understand your concern.
- Let's move to the next topic.
- Choose a topic of your interest.
- Find related information.
- Prepare a neat presentation.
- Add pictures to your project.
- Don't copy from the internet.
- Write in your own words.
- Check for errors.
- Submit it by Friday.
- Present your project confidently.
- Answer the questions asked.
- Maintain proper spacing in your writing.
- Don't rush through your work.
- Your calculation is incorrect.
- Please recheck the steps.
- Don't use a calculator for this question.
- Pay attention to punctuation.
- Use neat handwriting.

- Your answer is partially correct.
- This is the right approach.
- Try a different method.
- Who can give an example?
- What comes next?
- What is the meaning of this word?
- Can you frame a sentence?
- Which option is correct?
- Why did you choose that answer?
- Do you agree with him/her?
- That's a good suggestion.
- Let's look at another example.
- Anyone else?
- Treat others with kindness.
- Keep your promises.
- Share your things when needed.
- Don't hurt others' feelings.
- Say sorry if you make a mistake.
- Appreciate your classmates.
- Respect your teacher.
- Help someone who needs it.
- Don't speak rudely.
- Always be honest.
- Do not ask others for answers.
- Keep your eyes on your paper.
- Check your roll number.
- Don't leave early.
- Write all parts of the answer.
- Keep your handwriting legible.

- Use the extra time wisely.
- Don't panic.
- Read the question twice.
- Stay calm.
- Move to your assigned seat.
- Keep your bags on the rack.
- Form a line.
- Don't push anyone.
- Maintain silence in the corridor.
- Respect school property.
- Don't write on desks.
- Keep the classroom clean.
- Don't eat during class.
- Follow classroom etiquette.
- That is a brilliant idea.
- Let's solve this together.
- I appreciate your effort.
- Continue what you were doing.
- Note down the important points.
- Don't forget the deadline.
- You are almost correct.
- Let's correct it together.
- Don't hesitate to ask.
- I value your feedback.
- Interpret the data carefully.
- Provide a logical explanation.
- Compare the two methods.
- Support your answer with examples.
- Identify the key differences.

- Focus on accuracy rather than speed.
- Elaborate your points clearly.
- Don't jump to conclusions.
- Evaluate the solution critically.
- Summarize your understanding.
- What is your perspective on this?
- How can we apply this concept?
- What might be the consequences?
- Predict the next outcome.
- Analyze the cause and effect.
- Justify your opinion.
- Is your argument valid?
- How can you improve this answer?
- What assumptions are you making?
- Consider all possibilities before deciding.
- Rewrite the paragraph in your own style.
- Connect the ideas logically.
- Don't use informal language here.
- Focus on clarity and structure.
- Present your thoughts concisely.
- Avoid unnecessary repetition.
- Use formal academic tone.
- Refer to the example provided.
- Highlight the essential points.
- Compare your answer with the sample.
- Let's explore this concept further.
- Who can summarize the discussion?
- Can someone provide a counterargument?
- What evidence supports your claim?

- How is this idea relevant today?
- Let's evaluate both sides.
- That's a strong argument.
- Let's hear another viewpoint.
- What questions does this raise?
- How can we relate this to real life?
- Prepare a detailed report.
- Present your findings tomorrow.
- Work on improving your vocabulary.
- Use appropriate technical terms.
- Organize your project systematically.
- Add references to your information.
- Check for grammatical errors.
- Avoid plagiarism at all costs.
- Include diagrams wherever necessary.
- Provide a convincing conclusion.
- Your explanation lacks clarity.
- You need to expand your ideas.
- Your introduction is strong.
- This part needs more detail.
- Your logic is sound.
- The conclusion is well-written.
- Try to improve your presentation skills.
- Your writing shows improvement.
- Work on your grammar.
- Excellent critical thinking!
- Respect everyone's opinions.
- Maintain academic honesty.
- Keep your phones switched off.

- Participate actively in discussions.
- Maintain professionalism.
- Reflect on your learning.
- Treat the classroom as a shared space.
- Be mindful of your actions.
- Stay committed to your goals.
- Communicate respectfully.
- Form a circle for discussion.
- Arrange your desks neatly.
- Prepare for the next activity.
- Maintain a calm atmosphere.
- Don't distract others.
- Ensure everyone is included.
- Take turns speaking.
- Respect the time limit.
- Collaborate effectively.
- Contribute meaningfully.
- Let's revisit the previous topic.
- Connect this idea to what you already know.
- Keep track of important points.
- Make notes as you listen.
- Observe the pattern carefully.
- Identify the error in this sentence.
- Apply the formula correctly.
- Relate this concept to a real-life example.
- Read the passage with understanding.
- Break down the complex idea.
- Write a detailed analysis.
- Support your argument with facts.

- Compare and contrast the ideas.
- Provide meaningful insights.
- Use precise academic language.
- Present your answer in points.
- Avoid vague statements.
- Demonstrate deep understanding.
- Provide a structured explanation.
- Write a coherent essay.
- That was an impressive explanation.
- You have shown great improvement.
- Your ideas are original.
- You expressed your thoughts well.
- Your effort is remarkable.
- You have strong analytical skills.
- Keep exploring new ideas.
- You are developing confidence.
- Keep refining your skills.
- Aim for excellence.
- Do you agree with the interpretation?
- How does your idea differ?
- What is the significance of this?
- Can you clarify your statement?
- What conclusion can we draw?
- How can we apply this practically?
- What is the underlying concept?
- Does anyone have a different view?
- What leads you to this answer?
- Can you improve this explanation?
- Provide a real-world example.

- Explain the reasoning behind your answer.
- Evaluate the strengths and weaknesses.
- Compare your findings with the text.
- Analyze the pattern given.
- Identify the missing information.
- Let's verify the answer.
- Interpret the figure accurately.
- Discuss the impact of this issue.
- Suggest possible solutions.
- Summarize the key ideas.
- Share your personal insight.
- Organize your thoughts before speaking.
- Use supportive evidence.
- Maintain eye contact during the presentation.
- Stay focused throughout the lesson.
- Make a list of questions you have.
- Reflect on what you learned today.
- Prepare for tomorrow's quiz.
- Bring your materials for the project.
- Review your previous notes.
- Don't hesitate to ask doubts.
- Identify the main argument.
- Let's solve this step by step.
- Pay attention to the details.
- Stick to the topic while speaking.
- Don't repeat unnecessary points.
- Use appropriate examples.
- Avoid distractions.
- Respect the classroom environment.

- Keep your belongings safe.
- Use polite words with everyone.
- Pay attention to the board.
- Don't interrupt the speaker.
- Raise valid questions.
- Stay organized.
- Think deeply about this idea.
- Present your work neatly.
- Share your answer confidently.
- Don't worry about mistakes.
- Learning takes time.
- Make meaningful contributions.
- Keep your focus strong.
- Understand the concept fully.
- Help others when possible.
- Don't rush through your work.
- Ask for clarification.
- Apply what you learned.
- Be responsible for your work.
- Respect deadlines.
- Try to improve your accuracy.
- Make corrections carefully.
- Observe the changes closely.
- Use proper grammar.
- Read the paragraph slowly.
- Prepare a short summary.
- Write your thoughts clearly.
- Take pride in your work.
- Accept constructive feedback.

- Ask meaningful questions.
- Encourage your classmates.
- Stay curious.
- Try solving it independently.
- Don't depend on others' answers.
- Be confident in your ideas.
- Think creatively.
- Explore different strategies.
- Respect different viewpoints.
- Stay positive.
- Develop good study habits.
- Keep learning new things.
- Use time wisely.
- Challenge yourself.
- Believe in your abilities.
- Always try your best.
- Stay committed to improvement.
- Keep growing every day.
- Manoj is a brilliant student.
- He is a bright student.
- He is really on the ball.
- You are a natural boy.
- She doesn't miss a trick.
- Rahul is a very bright kid.
- She is very gifted.
- He is very clever at physics.
- You have got a gift for it.
- Peter is a highly intelligent boy.
- He is nobody's fool. (sensible and wise)

- He is quick off the mark.
- He is a bright spark.
- She is a bit of a goody-goody in the classroom.
- Your daughter is very smart and personable.
- He is a bit slow.
- Rahul is a slow learner.
- She can't put two and two together.
- He is as dumb as a past.
- She is a bit slow on the uptake.
- He is not the sharpest tool in the shed.
- How are you going to get home from school after class?
- Did you enjoy the weekend?
- See you on Monday.
- See you tomorrow.
- Enjoy your holiday.
- Have a good holiday.

3. DON'T KNOW

- I don't know the answer.
- If you don't know, ask me.
- I don't know this problem.
- I don't know how to solve this.
- I don't know how to do this.
- I don't know anything about it.
- I don't know what to do.
- Sorry I don't know what to say.

4. EXPRESSIONS FOR FORGETTING

- I forget to bring the note.

- I cannot remember.
- I do not memorize anything.
- My mind went blank.
- It completely slipped my mind.
- My memory is short.
- It went in one ear and out the other.
- I failed to remember.
- I am sorry. I forgot about it.
- I can't recall who said that.
- I cannot recall all their names.
- I failed to remember the method.

5. EXPRESSIONS FOR REMEMBERING

- Do you remember?
- I remember what you said.
- Now I remember.
- I will always remember.
- I will never forget.
- As I recall, it was you who suggested this idea.
- Now I come to think of it….

6. DON'T

- Don't move.
- Don't cheat.
- Don't come here.
- Don't shout.
- Don't show.
- Don't hide.
- Don't repeat the mistake.

- Don't make noise.
- Don't jump here.
- Don't waste your time.
- Don't talk here.
- Don't speak.
- Don't sleep.
- Don't move.
- Don't stand.
- Don't sit.
- Don't go.
- Don't be afraid.
- Don't feel.
- Don't cry.
- Don't touch anything.
- Don't throw.
- Don't sit idle.
- Don't hesitate.
- Don't interrupt.
- Don't run fast.
- Don't talk here, be quiet.
- Don't chew gum in the class.
- Don't throw anything.
- Don't go there.
- Don't do that.
- Don't do it again.
- Don't do this here.
- Don't choose this.
- Don't lift.
- Don't beat him.

- Don't tell lie.
- Don't say anything.
- Don't make me angry.
- Don't draw on the wall.
- Don't tease others.
- Don't argue.
- Don't cheat me.
- Don't continue this.
- Don't accept it.
- Don't forget to bring your note tomorrow.
- Don't make noise when you leave.
- Don't try my patience.
- Don't disturb your neighbor.
- Don't look out of the window.
- Don't behave like this.
- Don't push him.
- Don't pull.
- Don't blame others.
- Don't use bad words.
- Don't bother about it.
- Don't let him in.
- Don't disturb him.
- Don't walk on the grass.
- Don't write on the bench.
- Don't write on the wall.
- Don't bite your nails.
- Don't grit the teeth.
- Don't disturb.
- Don't insult others.

- Don't get upset.
- Don't get angry.
- Don't give excuses.
- Don't talk louder.
- Don't forget your homework.
- Don't joke.
- Don't be late for school.
- Don't be so childish.
- Don't be naughty.
- Don't be afraid.
- Don't be lazy.
- Don't be sad.
- Don't wait for me.
- Don't get nervous.
- Don't eat so fast.
- Don't gulp your food.
- Don't wander in the verandah.
- Don't talk about others.
- Don't stand on the bench.
- Don't sit on the floor.
- Don't play in the class.
- Don't read fast.
- Don't depend others.
- Don't follow others.
- Don't waste water.
- Don't spill water.
- Don't paste the cover.
- Don't ignore anything.
- Don't pair with others. Do it alone.

- Don't scribble on the wall.
- Don't shake the bench.
- Don't throw the paper.
- Don't be so negative.
- Don't forget to come in uniform.
- Don't make any noise as you leave.
- Don't tickle me.
- Don't be in hurry.
- Don't bite your nails.
- Don't miss new lessons.
- Don't make excuses.
- Don't argue with the teachers.

7. PROBLEM

- I am stuck on this problem, can you help me?
- Could you explain it in more detail?
- Can you help me with this problem?
- Would you help me to solve this problem?
- I cannot understand this.
- Can you explain something to me?

8. REPEAT / ASKING AGAIN

- Pardon.
- Could you say that once again, please?
- Could you repeat that, please?
- Can you please speak slowly?
- I am sorry, what did you say?
- Can you spell that word, please?

9. ASKING HELP

- Do you need help?
- Yes, please help me.
- I need your help.
- Can you help me, please?
- Would you please help me?
- Give me a hand, please.

10. SAY 'THANK YOU'

- Thank you.
- Thanks for your help.
- Thank you for reminding me.
- Thanks for your advice.
- Thanks for the gift.
- Thank you, I will try that.

11. LATE

- Why are you late?
- The bus was late.
- I had to wait for the bus.
- I was stuck in traffic.
- I got into a traffic jam.
- I missed the school bus.
- The traffic was terrible.

12. SAY 'SORRY'

- I am very sorry.
- Please forgive me.

- Sorry, it is my mistake.
- I am very sorry for what I did.
- I am sorry. I lost your pen.
- Sorry for being late again, Madam.

13. ENCOURAGE THE STUDENT

- Work hard
- Keep working on it. You are improving.
- Keep on trying.
- Why not give it a try?
- Come on! You can do it.
- Do your best.
- Go on Arun. You can do it.
- Take effort.
- There is nothing to fear.
- Nothing can stop you now.
- You handled that so well.
- I hope you can make it.
- Believe in yourself.
- I am proud of you.
- I am behind you.
- Never give up.
- I like your creativity.

14. IDENTIFICATION MARK

- A mole on right ear.
- A wound mark on left thigh.
- A scar left side of chin.
- Cut mark on left hand wrist.

- Birthmark on neck.
- Cut mark on forehead.
- Cut mark on chin.
- A tiny mole next to his nose.
- A mole on her neck.
- A black mole on her cheek.
- A scar on his right hand.
- A black mole on left arm.

15. TIME

- Excuse me, what time is it?
- Excuse me, time please.
- Could you tell me the time?
- May I know the time?
- What is the time now?
- What time do you make it?
- Do you have exact time?
- It is one o'clock.
- Is it four o'clock already?
- It's half past four.
- It is a quarter past four.
- It is five past nine.
- It is three past one.
- It's ten past eight.
- It's six o'clock.
- It is 8 pm already.
- It's 7:30.
- It's twenty past one.
- It's twenty-five past seven.

- It's twenty-five to three.
- It's twenty to eleven.
- It's ten to one.
- 1.00 – It is one o'clock.
- 1.05 – It is five (minutes) past one.
- 1:15 – It is (a) quarter past one. (one fifteen)
- 1:25 – It is twenty-five past one. (one twenty-five)
- 1:30 – It's half past one. (one thirty)
- 1:35 – It is twenty five to two. (one thirty-five)
- 1:45 – It is quarter to two. (one forty-five)
- 1:50 – It is ten to two. (one fifty)
- 1:57 – It is three (minutes) to two. (one fifty-seven)

16. AT STAFF ROOM

- I am a teacher.
- What do you teach?
- I teach English.
- He is a good teacher.
- I am in school.
- I am on my way to school.
- Stay in school.
- School begins at nine.
- School begins in June.
- You are early.
- How is the class today?
- I have no idea where my class is.
- I am not sure how to find my class.
- What building is it in?
- It is on the second floor.

- It is on D block.
- Do you have register?
- Do you have name list for your class?
- Do you want a name list?
- Where can I get the name list?
- I am going to change that.
- How long have you been working here?
- I have been working here for the past 10 years.
- Did you know that he has 15 years of teaching experience?
- Are you in his class?
- This guy was so funny when he was teaching.
- I am going to leave the class early.
- Why do you have to leave early?
- I am not feeling well.
- Can you stay for a few more minutes?
- Are you leaving right away?
- Sorry, I can't stay until the end of class.
- I have an appointment.
- I am leaving right now.
- Have you arranged for someone to take classes for you?
- What class would you like to take?
- Which class do you want?
- Do you know what class you want to take?
- On what days are the classes?
- The class is from nine to twelve on Saturday.
- Can you tell me about the other classes?
- Sir, I have a problem with my class timetable.
- I have two classes on that same time.
- Two of my classes occur at the same time.

- Is there any way that you can fix my class?
- Can you change that for me?
- Do you want those classes?
- Yes, I would like to keep both classes.
- Are you free now?
- Will you be free?
- Don't tell me how to do my job.
- It is not my decision.
- I have to obey my superiors.
- I know what you mean.
- I didn't say you took it.
- I just want to do my job.
- I don't know why it happened.
- Let's not discuss this now.
- There is something I have to say.
- I am not causing the problem.
- He quit school last week.
- He was expelled from school.
- Do you want to read this magazine?
- I didn't finish my lunch.
- You are going to be late again.
- Thank you for all the gifts.
- How did the exam go?
- How did you manage this?
- How did the rehearsal go?
- Do you have a pen or pencil?
- Don't put it on my desk.
- I don't have any classes today.
- Can you just give me a minute?

- When did you tell me that?
- I would come but I have work.
- I was a student in 2008.
- Now, I am going to my classroom.
- Are you free in the afternoon?
- I may have to give a speech.
- I am sorry for the delay.
- You may start exam now.
- Would you mind if I sit here?
- Consider my request.
- Ignore his request.
- The principal turned down my request.
- It appears to me that he is angry.
- I will arrange a meeting.
- Everything has been arranged.
- I want you to arrange the bench.
- We arranged the book according to size.
- I am gathering information.
- Students are gathering.
- Everybody was gathered in the smart room.
- The teacher gathered his students around her.
- The students assembled in the classroom.
- There are forty-five students in the assembly hall.
- Thank you for making the arrangements.
- He came at last.
- It appears to be working.
- I admit I am wrong.
- Students appeared on the stage.
- Split students into two teams.

- I only want to know the facts.
- Why are you waiting here?
- He looked at me in surprise.
- The word is not in my dictionary.
- That's not how you spell my name.
- I can't remember.
- Why is this place dirty?
- I don't want to read that book.
- I am too weak to do that.
- Don't you want to try something new?
- Did you understand any of that?
- Did you like that book?
- I want to read this book.
- What kind of books do you like?
- That's not my favourite topic.
- This is too difficult for me.
- What was the reason for that?
- I don't have many books.
- Tell me where you got it.
- When is the school bus leaving?
- Are you up for drinking coffee after class?
- Don't you have class?
- The girl was admitted to the hospital.
- Children under three are not admitted
- He was admitted to that school without taking the exam.
- I cannot accept that explanation.
- I accept full responsibility.
- He didn't attend the class.
- I took that class already.

- What other classes are you going to take?
- I arrived at school on time.
- They invited me to the marriage.
- I was not invited.
- Where is Anand?
- He is on his lunch break.
- He is in class.
- He is in a meeting.
- He is at work.
- He is at a conference.
- He has gone to meeting.
- School keeps me pretty busy.
- I go and consult with principal.
- Why are you so quiet?
- I am just worried about my students.
- Everybody at school hates me.
- Let's do it after school.
- We did it in school.
- School is over at 3:30.
- School is over now.
- Do you want to take bus?
- I will drive you to bus stop.
- No, let's foot it.
- I come to school by walking.
- I come to school at eight.
- They live near the school.
- I left school early.
- There is no school today.
- We have no school tomorrow.

- I am proud of my school.
- Did you take attendance today?
- I have a free period now.
- I have class next.
- Can I borrow your pen?
- Is the printer working?
- I need to photocopy this.
- Where is the register?
- Has the principal arrived?
- I will be in my classroom.
- Can you help me with this form?
- I need the chalk box.
- The meeting starts soon.
- Who has the key to the lab?
- Please pass the attendance sheet.
- Today's schedule is tight.
- I have extra papers in my drawer.
- Does anyone have a stapler?
- I will take the substitution period.
- I need to submit the report today.
- Is the projector available?
- Who is on duty today?
- I have to prepare the exam paper.
- The bell has rung.
- Let's go for assembly.
- I need to check the notebooks.
- Can you sign this?
- I will return it in a minute.
- The students are waiting for me.

- I have a meeting with parents.
- Can someone cover my class for 10 minutes?
- I will upload the lesson plan soon.
- Please share the timetable file.
- The internet is very slow today.
- I must complete the evaluation by evening.
- The principal wants the report immediately.
- I need to prepare for tomorrow's lesson.
- The test papers are ready for correction.
- Do we have any extra answer sheets?
- The photocopier is out of paper.
- Can anyone help me with the computer?
- The staff meeting is postponed.
- I will coordinate the event.
- Please send the circular to all classes.
- We need to update the attendance record.
- I have to supervise the exam hall.
- Let's discuss the new activity plan.
- The students performed well today.
- We need more materials for the project.
- The classroom needs cleaning.
- I need to speak with the principal later.
- Who will take the substitution for Grade 7?
- I am preparing for the cultural program.
- The syllabus is almost completed.
- I need one more week to finish the portion.
- Please check the circular before printing.
- Let's finalize the exam timetable.
- The parents are waiting in the office.

- I am sending the marks to the office.
- I need to arrange the files properly.
- Do we have extra stationery?
- The students were very active today.
- Can someone help me with the worksheet?
- I will conduct the special class today.
- Let's plan for next month's activities.
- Please share your feedback on the lesson.
- The new teacher will join next week.
- We need to coordinate for Annual Day.
- I am updating the attendance in the portal.
- The printer ink needs to be replaced.
- Let's collaborate on the lesson planning.
- Please update the records before submitting.
- We need to review the academic progress.
- Let's arrange a meeting with all department heads.
- The exam papers need to be moderated.
- We must ensure that all students are monitored.
- Please send me the digital copy of the syllabus.
- I'll prepare the report for the next meeting.
- The training session was very informative.
- Let's discuss ways to improve classroom engagement.
- The feedback form needs to be revised.
- We should plan a workshop for teachers.
- The annual report is almost complete.
- I need your approval for the lesson plan.
- Let's coordinate the field trip details.
- The assessment guidelines have changed.
- We must ensure timely completion of tasks.

- Let's divide the responsibilities equally.
- The new curriculum looks challenging.
- Please cross-check the student data.
- We need to improve communication with parents.
- The students need additional support classes.
- Let's discuss strategies for better discipline.
- Please verify the marks before uploading.
- We should organize a teacher development session.
- The management requested a detailed report.
- The staffroom needs better organization.
- Let's finalize the duty schedule for the event.
- I appreciate your cooperation.
- Let's work together to make the academic year successful.

17. PRINCIPAL OFFICE SENTENCES

- Good morning, madam.
- May I come in, sir?
- I need to meet the principal.
- The principal is in a meeting.
- Please wait for a few minutes.
- You may go inside now.
- The principal will see you now.
- Please sit down.
- What brings you here?
- Do you have an appointment?
- Please submit your application.
- I need your signature, madam.
- This file is for your approval.

- The principal is not available now.
- You can meet the principal later.
- Please come during office hours.
- The principal has called you.
- You are late for the meeting.
- Wait outside until you are called.
- Please submit your complaint here.
- Write your details in the register.
- The office staff will help you.
- Take this letter to your class teacher.
- The principal wants this report today.
- You must follow the school rules.
- Don't be nervous.
- Tell me your problem clearly.
- Are your parents here?
- Please maintain discipline.
- You can leave now.
- Why were you absent yesterday?
- Your attendance is very low.
- Please bring your parents tomorrow.
- You must improve your behaviour.
- This is your final warning.
- I expect better performance from you.
- Submit your project before the deadline.
- The school management needs this report.
- Please prepare the documents quickly.
- I need the updated student list.
- We have a staff meeting today.
- The principal wants all teachers to attend.

- Please share the circular with all classes.
- The timetable must be revised.
- The exam schedule needs approval.
- Please arrange a meeting with parents.
- We need to plan for the school event.
- Submit the monthly progress report.
- The principal has approved your request.
- The proposal needs further changes.
- Please explain the situation clearly.
- We must follow the school policies.
- This issue will be investigated.
- Thank you for bringing this to our notice.
- The principal will take action soon.
- Please cooperate with the investigation.
- We need additional documents from you.
- Prepare a clean copy of the letter.
- Your complaint will be forwarded.
- Please collect your ID card from the office.
- The office will contact your parents.
- You must follow the instructions given.
- This matter is very serious.
- We will discuss this in the next meeting.
- Please confirm your attendance.
- The decision will be announced tomorrow.
- Kindly wait for further information.
- Your request cannot be accepted now.
- Please submit the form again.
- Thank you, you may leave.
- Let's review the disciplinary report.

- We need to ensure transparency in this matter.
- Please provide a detailed explanation.
- Our priority is the safety of students.
- The management requires quick action.
- We must maintain the school's standards.
- Please update the records immediately.
- This issue must be resolved professionally.
- The school appreciates your cooperation.
- The final decision will be taken after discussion.
- Kindly submit the official documents.
- Your performance will be closely monitored.
- We expect complete honesty from everyone.
- The school encourages open communication.
- Please handle this situation carefully.
- We must follow all guidelines strictly.
- This matter requires urgent attention.
- Please prepare a detailed written report.
- The meeting minutes must be recorded properly.
- We value your contribution to the school.
- The new policy will start next month.
- All staff must follow the updated rules.
- Let's coordinate for the upcoming inspection.
- Prepare the documents for submission.
- Ensure accuracy before sending the report.
- Let's maintain a positive school environment.
- The principal appreciates your hard work.
- Thank you for your responsible efforts.
- You may return to your class now.
- Have a productive day.

18. SCHOOL OFFICE SENTENCES

- Good morning, how can I help you?
- Please wait for your turn.
- Write your name in the register.
- What is your class and section?
- Please submit your application here.
- Do you have any ID proof?
- Take this slip to your teacher.
- The office will open at 9 a.m.
- The principal is not available right now.
- You can collect it after lunch.
- Please sit and wait.
- Do you have an appointment?
- The photocopy machine is not working.
- Please visit again tomorrow.
- Your parents need to sign this form.
- Here is your receipt.
- Please pay the fees at the counter.
- Take your hall ticket from window number 2.
- The principal has called you.
- The office is closed during lunch break.
- Please fill out this form.
- Submit the filled form here.
- Bring two passport-size photos.
- Collect your ID card from the desk.
- Please provide your mobile number.
- Your uniform form is ready.
- Take the token and wait.

- You may collect your certificate on Friday.
- Please sign the register before leaving.
- The office staff will guide you.
- Please submit the fee receipt for verification.
- The admission form is available online.
- You must provide the correct documents.
- The office cannot accept incomplete forms.
- Please check the notice board for updates.
- The bus route details are available here.
- The office needs your signature on the declaration.
- Kindly update your address in our records.
- The certificates will be issued next week.
- Please attach a photocopy of your marksheet.
- The schedule for the meeting is ready.
- Collect your transfer certificate from the counter.
- Please read all instructions before submitting.
- We need your parent's consent letter.
- The office will send an SMS for confirmation.
- Please wait until your form is checked.
- The staff will inform you about the next step.
- Your complaint has been registered.
- The report will be forwarded to the principal.
- Please collect your refund from the accounts office.
- The admission list will be displayed tomorrow.
- You must submit your documents before the deadline.
- Please provide the original certificate for verification.
- Your request will be processed soon.
- Kindly bring your parent for verification.
- Please fill the form in capital letters.

- The office needs your signature here.
- We will notify you when it is ready.
- You must follow the school procedures.
- Please clear your dues at the accounts section.
- Please collect your books from the store room.
- This is the official school circular.
- Kindly check your details before submitting.
- The office will update your information system.
- Please submit the clearance form.
- Your ID card will be printed today.
- Please bring the original documents tomorrow.
- The office will help you with bus pass renewal.
- Your request has been approved.
- Please take a copy of the final report.
- Please ensure all documents are properly attested.
- Your application will be processed after verification.
- Kindly submit the digital copy of your certificate as well.
- The management requires additional information.
- Please check the updated guidelines on the website.
- All records must be updated before the inspection.
- You are requested to meet the principal regarding this matter.
- The office will maintain a record of your request.
- Kindly ensure the accuracy of the submitted data.
- Your file has been forwarded to the administration.
- The certificates will be issued after final approval.
- Please collect your migration certificate from the admin block.
- Your request cannot be accepted without proper documentation.
- The school office will send an official email shortly.
- We require your parent's authorization letter.

- The decision will be announced after the review meeting.
- Please provide the necessary supporting documents.
- You must follow the administrative process carefully.
- The office will confirm the status by tomorrow.
- Your refund request has been processed successfully.
- Please submit the revised form with corrections.
- The final list will be displayed on the notice board.
- Kindly ensure timely submission of all documents.
- Your attendance report is ready for collection.
- Please check your details in the portal.
- The office will verify your identity.
- You may collect the approved document now.
- The administration appreciates your cooperation.
- Please meet the vice-principal for further instructions.
- Have a nice day, and thank you for your patience.

19. PARENT-TEACHER MEETING

- Good morning, please come in.
- Please have a seat.
- What is your child's name?
- Which class is your child studying in?
- How can I help you today?
- Your child is doing well.
- Your child needs improvement.
- Your child is very active in class.
- Attendance is low this month.
- Your child must complete homework regularly.
- Please check the diary every day.
- Your child is improving slowly.

- Your child gets distracted easily.
- Please encourage reading at home.
- Your child behaves well in class.
- Your child needs more practice in writing.
- Your child needs help with English.
- Your child is weak in mathematics.
- Your child is good at sports.
- I appreciate your child's effort.
- Please make sure your child brings all books.
- Kindly sign the homework notebook.
- Encourage your child to participate in activities.
- Your child needs to follow classroom rules.
- Please speak to your child about discipline.
- Your support at home is important.
- Your child must come to school on time.
- Please reduce screen time at home.
- Your child needs more concentration.
- Thank you for visiting.
- Your child is showing good improvement this term.
- He participates well in group activities.
- Please motivate your child to ask questions.
- She is a responsible student.
- Your child needs more confidence in speaking.
- He must complete classwork regularly.
- Please encourage your child to revise daily.
- Your child needs guidance in time management.
- He sometimes forgets homework.
- Your child needs to improve handwriting.
- She is respectful and polite.

- Your child must focus during explanations.
- I suggest extra reading practice at home.
- Please monitor your child's study habits.
- He needs more support with assignments.
- Your child is doing well in tests.
- She finds some topics challenging.
- Please check the notebook regularly.
- Encourage your child to speak in English.
- Your child needs to work on problem-solving skills.
- He/she must revise before exams.
- Please ensure your child brings stationery.
- Your child must avoid talking in class.
- He needs to follow directions carefully.
- I appreciate your child's creativity.
- Behaviour has improved this month.
- He is helpful and cooperative.
- Please motivate regular study habits.
- Your child must avoid last-minute studying.
- He should participate more in class discussions.
- Let's work together for your child's progress.
- He needs more practice in reading comprehension.
- Your child must attend extra classes.
- Please support your child emotionally as well.
- She is capable of better performance.
- Your child completes tasks with guidance.
- Please encourage independent learning.
- Kindly limit mobile phone usage.
- Let's set goals for the next month.
- Thank you for cooperating with us.

- Your child has shown consistent academic growth.
- He demonstrates strong critical thinking skills.
- We need to address the behavioral concerns.
- Your child is very talented but needs discipline.
- Let’s work on building study habits at home.
- Your child has difficulty concentrating for long periods.
- I recommend additional support for this subject.
- She expresses ideas clearly during discussions.
- Please encourage your child to manage time effectively.
- Your child needs to balance academics and activities.
- He must take responsibility for learning.
- Your child needs help organizing school materials.
- Let’s focus on improving test performance.
- I suggest regular revision and reading practice.
- Your child benefits from individual attention.
- Your son needs to improve listening skills.
- Your child is capable of excellent results with effort.
- Please maintain regular communication with the school.
- Your daughter has great potential but needs motivation.
- Let's create a plan to support your child.
- Your child behaves well with teachers and students.
- We need to work on consistent homework completion.
- He must avoid distractions during lessons.
- Please monitor your child's progress regularly.
- Your child learns quickly with proper guidance.
- Let’s aim for steady improvement in all subjects.
- I appreciate your involvement in your child’s learning.
- He is improving academically and emotionally.
- Thank you for working with us for your child’s success.

- Feel free to contact me anytime for updates.

20. PT PERIOD

- Good morning, students.
- Stand in a straight line.
- Keep some distance between each other.
- Start your warm-up exercises.
- Move your hands up and down.
- Stretch your legs properly.
- Don't bend your back.
- Do it slowly and correctly.
- Now start jogging.
- Run on the track only.
- Don't push anyone while running.
- Keep your speed steady.
- Stop and take a deep breath.
- Drink water if you feel tired.
- Today we will practice drills.
- Follow the instructions carefully.
- Maintain discipline.
- Listen when I am speaking.
- Don't talk in the line.
- Pay attention to your posture.
- Now we will start skipping.
- Try to jump higher.
- Relax your muscles.
- Sit down for a few minutes.
- Now stand up slowly.
- We will practice for sports day.

- Give your best in every activity.
- Teamwork is important.
- Help each other and play fair.
- Don't complain unnecessarily.
- If you get hurt, tell me immediately.
- Never cheat during games.
- Respect your teammates.
- Respect your opponents too.
- Always keep your body active.
- Practice makes you better.
- You must improve your stamina.
- Cool down after exercising.
- Great job, everyone!
- See you all in the next PT period.
- PT sir, may I join the class?
- PT sir, what are we doing today?
- PT sir, am I doing this correctly?
- PT sir, can you please repeat the step?
- PT sir, I completed my rounds.
- Sir, may I take some rest?
- Sir, I am feeling tired.
- PT sir, I need a water break.
- PT sir, my leg is hurting.
- PT sir, please check my posture.
- PT sir, how many laps should we run?
- PT sir, can I try again?
- PT sir, when is our next practice?
- PT sir, I want to join the team.
- PT sir, please teach me the correct technique.

- PT sir, can we play a game today?
- PT sir, I forgot the rule.
- PT sir, please explain it again.
- Sir, is this the right way?
- Sir, thank you for helping me.
- Sir, sorry, I made a mistake.
- PT sir, I will do better next time.
- Sir, I want to improve my speed.
- PT sir, can you tell me my score?
- PT sir, am I in the team?
- PT sir, may I go drink water?
- PT sir, my shoe lace is open.
- PT sir, can I tie my shoe?
- PT sir, can we have a warm-up game?
- PT sir, can you show that again?
- PT sir, I am ready for the next activity.
- Sir, should I stand here?
- PT sir, who is my partner?
- PT sir, may I lead the line?
- Sir, I want to participate in running.
- Sir, I want to participate in long jump.
- Sir, I want to participate in relay.
- PT sir, please mark my attendance.
- PT sir, thank you for the class.
- Our PT sir is very kind.
- PT sir teaches us exercise every day.
- PT sir keeps us active and healthy.
- He trains us for sports day.
- PT sir encourages everyone equally.

- He teaches us new games.
- PT sir is very disciplined.
- He motivates us to stay fit.
- PT sir always comes on time.
- He teaches us the value of teamwork.
- PT sir helps us when we get hurt.
- He maintains the sports equipment.
- PT sir teaches us yoga sometimes.
- He makes the class fun and energetic.
- PT sir tells us to never give up.
- He teaches us to play fair.
- He explains the rules clearly.
- He supports slow learners patiently.
- PT sir cheers for us during sports events.

21. Library

- Where is the library?
- Can I borrow this book?
- When should I return it?
- This is our library.
- I am in the library.
- The library is big.
- I like the library.
- I read books in the library.
- The library is quiet.
- I go to the library every day.
- There are many books here.
- I borrowed a book.
- I returned the book.
- The librarian is helpful.
- Please be quiet in the library.
- I found my book.
- The library is clean.
- I enjoy reading here.
- Our school has a beautiful library.
- I visit the library during breaks.
- The library has books on many subjects.
- I borrowed a storybook today.
- The librarian helped me choose a book.
- Students must follow library rules.
- I use my library card regularly.
- The books are arranged neatly.
- Reading in the library improves my knowledge.

- I spend my free time in the library.
- The library is my favourite place at school.
- I often read magazines in the library.
- The library opens early in the morning.
- I like exploring new books.
- The reading area is comfortable.
- I am going to the library.
- The library is open now.
- Let's study in the library.
- I borrowed a book from the library.
- Please return the book to the library.
- Our school library is very big.
- I spend time in the library every day.
- The library has many interesting books.
- We should keep silence in the library.
- The librarian helped me find a book.
- I need to visit the library after class.
- The library opens at 9 a.m.
- The library closes at 4 p.m.
- I got a library card today.
- Can you come to the library with me?
- We have a reading period in the library.
- The library is my favourite place in school.
- I borrowed a science book from the library.
- Students must follow library rules.
- The library is on the first floor.
- I returned my books to the library.
- The librarian is arranging the books.
- There are many storybooks in the library.

- We can improve our knowledge in the library.
- The library is quiet and peaceful.
- I found the book I wanted in the library.
- Our teacher took us to the library.
- The library has a computer section.
- I read newspapers in the library.
- Do you have this book in the library?
- How many books can I borrow at a time?
- What are the library timings?
- Can you help me find this book?
- Which section is this book in?
- May I renew this book?
- Is the library open today?
- Is the library open now?
- When does the library open?
- When does the library close?
- Can I go to the library now?
- May I enter the library?
- Is this the library?
- Can I sit here and read?
- Do you have storybooks?
- Where can I find books?
- Can I borrow this book?
- How many books can I borrow?
- When should I return this book?
- Do I need a library card?
- Who is the librarian?
- Can you help me find a book?
- Where is the science section?

- Where is the English section?
- Do you have this book?
- Is this book available?
- Can I take this book home?
- Can I renew this book?
- How long can I keep this book?
- Is there a fine for late returns?
- Can I reserve this book?
- Where should I return the books?
- Are newspapers available here?
- Do you have magazines?
- Can I use the computer in the library?
- Is there a reading room?
- Which book do you recommend?
- Do you have books for my project?
- Where can I find reference books?
- Are there any new books in the library?
- Can I borrow books during holidays?
- Is there a limit on borrowing books?
- Can students visit the library during lunch break?
- Are group discussions allowed here?
- Can I photocopy pages from this book?
- Is Wi-Fi available in the library?
- How can I improve my reading habits using the library?
- Which section contains books on general knowledge?
- Can you guide me to resources for my research project?
- What are the library rules and regulations?
- How do I search for a book in the library catalog?
- Are digital resources available in the library?

- Can I access online journals through the library?
- What should I do if I lose a library book?
- How often are new books added to the library?
- What are the benefits of using the library regularly?
- What kind of books do you read?
- Which is your favourite book in the library?
- What did you borrow from the library today?
- What do you usually do in the library?
- How can the library improve your knowledge?

22. Science Laboratory

- Sir/Madam, may I enter the lab?
- Can you explain the experiment again?
- I don't understand this step.
- Can you help me with this activity?
- What should I do next?
- How do I use this instrument?
- Can you check my observation?
- Is my answer correct?
- Could you please repeat the instructions?
- Where can I find the materials?
- I am ready to start the experiment.
- Let us begin the activity.
- I need a test tube.
- Please pass me the beaker.
- I am measuring the liquid.
- I am observing the reaction.
- The color is changing.

- I can see bubbles forming.
- The solution is becoming clear.
- The experiment is working.
- I am recording the observations.
- Let me write down the results.
- We are working as a team.
- Our group has completed the experiment.
- We got the expected result.
- I noticed a colour change.
- The temperature increased.
- The temperature decreased.
- The liquid started boiling.
- The reaction was very fast.
- The reaction was slow.
- I observed a chemical change.
- The sample looks different now.
- We obtained the same result.
- Our observations match the theory.
- I am wearing my lab coat.
- We must follow safety rules.
- Please handle the equipment carefully.
- Do not touch the chemicals directly.
- Keep the lab table clean.
- We should be careful with glassware.
- Safety goggles are important.
- Let us clean the equipment after use.
- We should not run in the lab.
- Please dispose of the waste properly.
- May I use the microscope?

- Can I borrow a ruler?
- Our experiment is successful.
- We need more water.
- I have completed my work.
- Let us compare our results.
- Please write your observations.
- The lab is very interesting.
- I like practical classes.
- Science is fun in the lab.
- This is our science lab.
- I am in the science lab.
- The lab is clean.
- We are doing an experiment.
- Please wear your lab coat.
- The teacher is in the lab.
- I need a test tube.
- Pass me the beaker, please.
- Be careful with the equipment.
- The experiment is interesting.
- I can see many instruments.
- The lab is well organized.
- Let's start the experiment.
- Please follow the instructions.
- The result is correct.
- We learn science in the laboratory.
- The teacher explained the experiment clearly.
- I am observing the reaction carefully.
- Please handle the chemicals safely.
- We are working in groups.

- The microscope is on the table.
- I recorded the observations.
- The experiment was successful.
- We should keep the lab clean.
- Safety rules are important in the lab.
- I enjoy practical science classes.
- The equipment should be used properly.
- We measured the liquid accurately.
- Everyone must wear safety glasses.
- The lab assistant helped us.
- What experiment are we doing today?
- Can you pass me the test tube?
- How should we use this equipment?
- What is the purpose of this experiment?
- Is it safe to touch this chemical?
- Can you explain this procedure again?
- What did you observe?
- Why did the color change?
- How do we record the results?
- What conclusion can we draw from this experiment?
- I learned something new today.
- This experiment was interesting.
- The science lab helps me understand concepts better.
- I enjoyed doing this practical activity.
- The experiment helped me understand the lesson clearly.
- The experiment helped us understand the topic clearly.
- Today we are studying cells.
- I am preparing a slide.
- Please pass me the microscope.

- I can see the nucleus clearly.
- Let me adjust the focus.
- This specimen is very interesting.
- I am observing the cell structure.
- Can you explain this diagram?
- I have recorded my observations.
- The slide is ready for observation.
- We are studying plant cells today.
- I can identify the cell wall.
- The specimen is visible under the microscope.
- This practical is very useful.
- We are learning about tissues.
- The experiment was successful.
- Please handle the slide carefully.
- I have completed the practical work.
- Biology is easier through experiments.
- I can distinguish between plant and animal cells.
- The observation matches the theory.
- We are studying the human body system.
- The microscope image is clear.
- I learned something new today.
- Today we are studying leaves.
- This is a plant specimen.
- I am observing the root system.
- The leaf veins are clearly visible.
- Can you identify this plant?
- We are studying plant anatomy.
- The flower has colourful petals.
- I am drawing the specimen.

- The plant tissue is visible.
- Let us examine the stem section.
- The roots absorb water from the soil.
- We are learning about photosynthesis.
- The specimen is fresh.
- I can identify the plant parts.
- The practical helped me understand the topic.
- This plant belongs to the flowering group.
- We are observing seed germination.
- The diagram is easy to understand.
- I have labeled all the parts.
- Botany is an interesting subject.
- The plant sample is healthy.
- Let us compare the specimens.
- The flower structure is unique.
- We observed different types of leaves.
- I enjoyed today's practical session.
- Today we are studying animal tissues.
- This specimen belongs to an insect.
- I am observing the animal structure.
- The specimen is preserved carefully.
- Can you identify this organism?
- We are studying the digestive system.
- The skeleton is clearly visible.
- I can see the different organs.
- Let us observe the specimen closely.
- The practical was very informative.
- We are learning animal classification.
- The specimen shows important features.

- I recorded my observations carefully.
- The microscope helped us study details.
- We are studying vertebrates and invertebrates.
- This animal belongs to the mammal group.
- The body structure is fascinating.
- I can identify the external features.
- Zoology practicals are very interesting.
- The observation supports the theory.
- We learned about the circulatory system.
- The specimen is displayed properly.
- I completed the diagram neatly.
- We compared different animal groups.
- The practical improved my understanding.
- Today we are conducting a physics experiment.
- Please pass me the meter scale.
- I am measuring the length accurately.
- The apparatus is working properly.
- Let me note down the readings.
- We are studying the laws of motion.
- The result is correct.
- I verified the measurements.
- The experiment was successful.
- We are calculating the final result.
- The reading should be accurate.
- I am using a stopwatch.
- The object moved with constant speed.
- We are studying electricity today.
- Please connect the circuit carefully.
- The bulb is glowing.

- The current is flowing through the wire.
- The voltage reading is correct.
- We are studying magnetic effects.
- The graph shows the relationship clearly.
- Physics experiments make concepts easier.
- We must handle the equipment carefully.
- I understood the principle behind the experiment.
- Practical work improves our learning.
- The physics lab helps us connect theory with practice.
- What is the aim of today's experiment?
- Can you explain the procedure once again?
- What materials do we need?
- What did you observe?
- How do we calculate the result?
- Is my observation correct?
- What conclusion can we draw?
- Can I use this microscope?
- Where should I record my observations?
- Have we completed the experiment?
- What is the purpose of this practical?
- Can you check my work, please?

23. Question Answers

- What is your name?
  My name is Arun.

- Which class do you study in?
  I study in Class 8.

- What is your roll number?
  My roll number is 15.

- Who is your class teacher?
  Mrs. Priya is my class teacher.

- What is your school name?
  My school name is ABC School.

- What time does school start?
  School starts at 9 a.m.

- What time does school end?
  School ends at 4 p.m.

- Do you come to school daily?
  Yes, I come daily.

- Are you late today?
  No, I am not late.

- Did you complete your homework?
  Yes, I completed it.

- Did you bring your notebook?
  Yes, I brought it.

- Did you bring your pen?
  Yes, I brought my pen.

- Can you read English?
  Yes, I can read English.

- Can you write neatly?
  Yes, I can write neatly.

- Can you answer this question?
  Yes, I can answer it.

- Do you like English class?
  Yes, I like English class.

- Which subject do you like most?
  I like Science most.

- Which subject is difficult for you?
  Mathematics is difficult for me.

- Who is absent today?
  Ravi is absent today.

- Who is your best friend?
  Karthik is my best friend.

- Where is your classroom?
  It is on the first floor.

- How many students are in your class?
  There are 40 students.

- Do you sit in the first row?
  Yes, I sit in the first row.

- What is today's date?
  Today is May 26.

- What day is today?
  Today is Tuesday.

- Did you study for the test?
  Yes, I studied well.

- Are you ready for the exam?
  Yes, I am ready.

- What did you learn today?
  I learned grammar today.

- Do you understand the lesson?
  Yes, I understand it.

- Do you have any doubts?
  No, I do not have doubts.

- Can you spell "zebra"?
  Z-E-B-R-A.

- Can you speak English?
  Yes, a little.

- What is your favourite book?
  My favourite book is a storybook.

- Do you visit the library?
  Yes, I visit the library.

- Which game do you play at school?
  I play cricket.

- Do you wear school uniform?
  Yes, I wear school uniform.

- What colour is your uniform?
  It is blue and white.

- Who is your principal?
  Mr. Kumar is our principal.

- Do you like your teachers?
  Yes, I like my teachers.

- What is your favourite classroom activity?
  Reading is my favourite activity.

- Did you eat lunch?
  Yes, I ate lunch.

- What did you bring for lunch?
  I brought lemon rice.

- Do you share your lunch?
  Yes, I share my lunch.

- Can you draw pictures?
  Yes, I can draw pictures.

- Which language do you speak at school?
  I speak English at school.

- Do you participate in sports?
  Yes, I participate in sports.

- Have you won any prizes?
  Yes, I won a prize in drawing.

- What is your favourite sport?
  My favourite sport is football.

- Do you sing songs at school?
  Yes, I sing songs.

- Can you dance?
  Yes, I can dance.

- What is your favourite colour?
  My favourite colour is green.

- What is your favourites food?
  My favourite food is dosa.

- What is your favourite fruit?
  My favourite fruit is mango.

- What is your favourite animal?
  My favourite animal is elephant.

- Do you like computer class?
  Yes, I like computer class.

- Can you use a computer?
  Yes, I can use a computer.

- What do you do during break time?
  I play with friends.

- Do you help your classmates?
  Yes, I help them.

- Are your classmates friendly?
  Yes, they are friendly.

- Who sits next to you?
  Rahul sits next to me.

- Do you like group activities?
  Yes, I like them.

- What is your favourite poem?
  My favourite poem is "Twinkle Twinkle."

- Can you recite a poem?
  Yes, I can recite a poem.

- What is your favourite song?
  My favourite song is a school song.

- Did you attend assembly today?
  Yes, I attended assembly.

- Who leads the prayer?
  Meena leads the prayer.

- Do you keep your classroom clean?
  Yes, I keep it clean.

- Can you clean the blackboard?
  Yes, I can clean it.

- What is written on the board?
  A grammar lesson is written.

- Did the teacher give homework?
  Yes, the teacher gave homework.

- Do you like teamwork?
  Yes, I like teamwork.

- Which teacher teaches Maths?
  Mr. Raj teaches Maths.

- Which teacher teaches Science?
  Mrs. Devi teaches Science.

- What is your favourite school event?
  Sports Day is my favourite event.

- Did you attend Sports Day?
  Yes, I attended it.

- Can you run fast?
  Yes, I can run fast.

- Do you like morning assembly?
  Yes, I like it.

- What do you do after school?
  I do my homework.

- Do you go to tuition?
  Yes, I go to tuition.

- What time do you wake up?
  I wake up at 6 a.m.

- What time do you sleep?
  I sleep at 10 p.m.

- Do you revise lessons daily?
  Yes, I revise daily.

- Can you solve Maths problems?
  Yes, I can solve them.

- What is your favourite chapter?
  My favourite chapter is "The Tiger."

- Do you ask questions in class?
  Yes, I ask questions.

- Are you shy in class?
  No, I am not shy.

- Do you listen to the teacher carefully?
  Yes, I listen carefully.

- Can you read aloud?
  Yes, I can read aloud.

- Do you enjoy school trips?
  Yes, I enjoy them.

- Have you gone on a school trip?
  Yes, I have gone.

- What did you learn in Science today?
  I learned about plants.

- What did you learn in Maths today?
  I learned fractions.

- What did you learn in English today?
  I learned new words.

- What is your favourite classroom game?
  Quiz games are my favourite.

- Do you play chess at school?
  Yes, I play chess.

- Are you good at drawing?
  Yes, I am good at drawing.
- Can you colour neatly?
  Yes, I can colour neatly.
- What do you write with?
  I write with a pen.
- Do you sharpen your pencil?
  Yes, I sharpen it.
- Is your bag heavy?
  Yes, it is heavy.
- Do you keep your books neatly?
  Yes, I keep them neatly.
- Have you finished your classwork?
  Yes, I finished it.
- What is your favourite school memory?
  Playing with friends is my favourite memory.
- Do you like school holidays?
  Yes, I like school holidays.
- Which festival is celebrated at school?
  Independence Day is celebrated.
- Can you give a speech?
  Yes, I can give a speech.
- Have you participated in competitions?
  Yes, I have participated.

- What competition do you like most?
  I like quiz competitions most.

- Do you like handwriting practice?
  Yes, I like it.

- Can you read storybooks?
  Yes, I can read storybooks.

- What is your favourite cartoon?
  Doraemon is my favourite cartoon.

- Do you play indoor games?
  Yes, I play indoor games.

- What is your favourite indoor game?
  Chess is my favourite indoor game.

- What is your favourite outdoor game?
  Cricket is my favourite outdoor game.

- Do you carry a water bottle?
  Yes, I carry one.

- Do you drink enough water?
  Yes, I drink enough water.

- Do you like exams?
  No, I do not like exams.

- Which exam is easy for you?
  English exam is easy for me.

- Which exam is hard for you?
  Maths exam is hard for me.

- Do you get good marks?
  Yes, I get good marks.

- What is your aim in life?
  I want to become an engineer.

- Can you use the dictionary?
  Yes, I can use it.

- What do you do in computer lab?
  I learn typing.

- Have you planted trees at school?
  Yes, I have planted trees.

- Do you like environmental activities?
  Yes, I like them.

- What do you do in the playground?
  I play football.

- Do you respect your teachers?
  Yes, I respect them.

- Do you obey school rules?
  Yes, I obey the rules.

- Can you help weak students?
  Yes, I can help them.

- What do you do before exams?
  I revise my lessons.

- Do you make notes?
  Yes, I make notes.

- Can you work in teams?
  Yes, I can work in teams.

- What is your favourite classroom seat?
  I like the front seat.

- Do you enjoy art class?
  Yes, I enjoy art class.

- What do you draw in art class?
  I draw nature pictures.

- Have you visited the science lab?
  Yes, I have visited it.

- What do you do in the science lab?
  I do experiments.

- Do you like experiments?
  Yes, I like experiments.

- Can you count from 1 to 100?
  Yes, I can count.

- Do you know multiplication tables?
  Yes, I know them.

- Can you read maps?
  Yes, I can read maps.

- What is your favourite place in school?
  The playground is my favourite place.

- Do you like school assembly songs?
  Yes, I like them.

- Who is your favourite friend in class?
  Suresh is my favourite friend.

- Can you speak on stage?
  Yes, I can speak on stage.

- Do you like school competitions?
  Yes, I like them.

- Have you acted in a drama?
  Yes, I have acted.

- What role did you play?
  I played a teacher role.

- Do you write with your right hand?
  Yes, I write with my right hand.

- Can you solve puzzles?
  Yes, I can solve puzzles.

- Do you like quizzes?
  Yes, I like quizzes.

- Do you know antonyms?
  Yes, I know antonyms.

- Do you know synonyms?
  Yes, I know synonyms.

- Can you form sentences?
  Yes, I can form sentences.

- Do you like storytelling?
  Yes, I like storytelling.

- Can you tell a story?
  Yes, I can tell a story.

- What is your favourite story?
  The Lion and the Mouse is my favourite story.

- Do you keep silence in class?
  Yes, I keep silence.

- What do you do during lunch break?
  I eat with friends.

- Can you share your books?
  Yes, I can share them.

- What do teachers teach?
  Teachers teach lessons.

- Why do you go to school?
  I go to learn.

- Do you enjoy learning?
  Yes, I enjoy learning.

- What do you write on?
  I write on paper.

- What is in your school bag?
  Books and notebooks are in my bag.

- Can you erase the board?
  Yes, I can erase it.

- What is your favourite classroom game?
  Word games are my favourite.

- What do you do after assembly?
  I go to class.

- Do you like discipline?
  Yes, I like discipline.

- Are you happy at school?
  Yes, I am happy at school.

- What do you do when the bell rings?
  I go to the next class.

- Can you follow instructions?
  Yes, I can follow instructions.

- What do you do in free periods?
  I read books.

- Do you carry an ID card?
  Yes, I carry it.

- What is your favourite school day?
  Friday is my favourite school day.

- Do you wear shoes to school?
  Yes, I wear shoes.

- Can you tie your shoelaces?
  Yes, I can tie them.

- What do you do before entering class?
  I greet the teacher.

- Can you introduce yourself?
  Yes, I can introduce myself.

- What is your favourite activity period?
  PT period is my favourite.

- Do you like learning new words?
  Yes, I like learning new words.

- What is your favourite English activity?
  Speaking practice is my favourite.

- Can you ask questions in English?
  Yes, I can ask questions.

- Do you read newspapers?
  Yes, I read newspapers.

- What do you do in the morning at school?
  I attend assembly.

- Do you like classroom discussions?
  Yes, I like discussions.

- Can you answer quickly?
  Yes, I can answer quickly.

- Do you keep your desk clean?
  Yes, I keep it clean.

- What do you learn from school?
  I learn discipline and knowledge.

- Can you work hard?
  Yes, I can work hard.

- What makes you happy at school?
  Friends make me happy.

- Do you thank your teachers?
  Yes, I thank them.

- Are you proud of your school?
  Yes, I am proud of my school.

- Do you enjoy studying?
  Yes, I enjoy studying.

- Why are you late to class?
  The bus was delayed.

- Why did you not complete your homework?
  I was not feeling well.

- Why are you talking in class?
  Sorry, teacher.

- Why is your uniform dirty?
  It got dirty on the way.

- Why did you come without books?
  I forgot them at home.

- Why are you sleeping in class?
  I slept late yesterday.

- Why did you miss school yesterday?
  I had a fever.

- Why are you making noise?
  Sorry, I will be quiet.

- Why did you not bring your ID card?
  I forgot it at home.

- Why are you not listening to the teacher?
  Sorry, teacher.

- Why is your homework incomplete?
  I did not understand the lesson.

- Why are you running in the corridor?
  I was getting late.

- Why did you fight with your friend?
  We had a misunderstanding.

- Why are you disturbing the class?
  Sorry, I will not do it again.

- Why is your notebook untidy?
  I wrote in a hurry.

- Why are you using your phone in class?
  I am sorry, teacher.

- Why did you not attend assembly?
  I came late to school.

- Why are you laughing during the lesson?
  Sorry, teacher.

- Why did you throw paper on the floor?
  I forgot to use the dustbin.

- Why are you out of the classroom?
  The teacher sent me out.

- Why did you copy in the test?
  I was afraid of failing.

- Why did you break the classroom rule?
  I made a mistake.

- Why are you not wearing proper shoes?
  My shoes are damaged.

- Why did you not submit your project?
  I could not finish it on time.

- Why are you absent so often?
  I have health problems.

- Why are you eating during class?
  I was hungry.

- Why did you push your classmate?
  It happened by mistake.

- Why are you shouting in class?
  Sorry, I got excited.

- Why did you not bring your lunch?
  I forgot it at home.

- Why are you drawing on the desk?
  I am sorry, teacher.

- Why did you tear the book?
  It happened accidentally.

- Why are you not in uniform today?
  My uniform is being washed.

- Why did you leave the classroom without permission?
  I had to go urgently.

- Why are you teasing other students?
  Sorry, I will stop.

- Why did you not study for the exam?
  I was sick.

- Why are you wasting time?
  I will finish my work now.

- Why are your marks low?
  I need more practice.

- Why did you forget your homework?
  I left it on the table.

- Why are you writing on the wall?
  Sorry, I will clean it.

- Why are you not paying attention?
  I was distracted.

- Why did you come late after lunch break?
  I was in the restroom.

- Why did you damage school property?
  It was an accident.

- Why are you not sitting properly?
  Sorry, teacher.

- Why are you making fun of others?
  I did not mean to hurt anyone.

- Why did you not follow instructions?
  I did not hear properly.

- Why are you playing during study time?
  Sorry, teacher.

- Why did you not answer the question?
  I did not know the answer.

- Why are you keeping the classroom dirty?
  I will clean it now.

- Why did you skip the class?
  I was not feeling well.

- Why are you arguing with your classmates?
  We had different opinions.

- How many marks did you get?
  I got 85 marks.

- Why are your marks low?
  I did not prepare well.

- Did you pass the exam?
  Yes, I passed the exam.

- What is your highest mark?
  My highest mark is 95.

- Which subject did you score highest in?
  I scored highest in English.

- Which subject did you score lowest in?
  I scored lowest in Maths.

- Are you happy with your marks?
  Yes, I am happy.

- Did you improve your marks this time?
  Yes, I improved a lot.

- Why did you fail in the test?
  I did not study properly.

- How can you improve your marks?
  I can study harder.

- Did you get full marks?
  No, I did not get full marks.

- What is your average mark?
  My average mark is 80.

- Who got the highest mark in class?
  Ravi got the highest mark.

- Did you study before the exam?
  Yes, I studied well.

- Why are your science marks low?
  I found the paper difficult.

- What mark did you get in English?
  I got 90 in English.

- What mark did you get in Maths?
  I got 75 in Maths.

- Are your parents happy with your marks?
  Yes, they are happy.

- Did your teacher praise your marks?
  Yes, my teacher praised me.

- Do you want higher marks next time?
  Yes, I want higher marks.

- How many marks are needed to pass?
  35 marks are needed to pass.

- Did you write all the answers?
  Yes, I wrote all the answers.

- Why did you lose marks?
  I made spelling mistakes.

- Did you complete the exam on time?
  Yes, I completed it on time.

- Which exam was easy for you?
  English exam was easy for me.

- Which exam was difficult for you?
  Maths exam was difficult for me.

- Did you get rank in class?
  Yes, I got second rank.

- How do you feel about your result?
  I feel happy about it.

- What will you do to score better?
  I will practice daily.

- Did you revise before the test?
  Yes, I revised properly.

- Why did you make mistakes in the exam?
  I was nervous.

- Did you answer all the questions?
  Yes, I answered all questions.

- What grade did you get?
  I got Grade A.

- Are you satisfied with your result?
  Yes, I am satisfied.

- Did you compare your marks with friends?
  Yes, I compared them.

- Who helped you score good marks?
  My teacher helped me.

- Do you like weekly tests?
  Yes, they help me learn.

- What is your target mark?
  My target is 100 marks.

- Did you get better marks than last time?
  Yes, I did.

- Why are exam marks important?
  They show our performance.

- Did you practice old question papers?
  Yes, I practiced them.

- What subject needs more improvement?
  Maths needs more improvement.

- Did you feel confident during the exam?
  Yes, I felt confident.

- What did your parents say about your marks?
  They appreciated me.

- Are marks important for success?
  Yes, marks are important.

- Did you attend all revision classes?
  Yes, I attended all classes.

- What mark did you expect?
  I expected 90 marks.

- Why are you disappointed with your marks?
  I expected more marks.

- Do you study every day?
  Yes, I study daily.

- Will you work harder next exam?
  Yes, I will work harder.

- Why did you fight with your classmate?
  We had an argument.

- Who started the fight?
  He started the fight.

- Did you hit your friend?
  No, I did not hit him.

- Why were you angry?
  He took my pen.

- Did you say sorry after the fight?
  Yes, I said sorry.

- What happened during the fight?
  We shouted at each other.
- Did the teacher see the fight?
  Yes, the teacher saw it.
- Why did you push your friend?
  It happened by mistake.
- Did your friend hurt you?
  No, he did not hurt me.
- Are you still angry with him?
  No, I am not angry now.
- Did you complain to the teacher?
  Yes, I complained.
- Why were you shouting in class?
  We were arguing.
- Did you break anything during the fight?
  No, nothing broke.
- Did your parents know about the fight?
  Yes, they know.
- Why did your friend get angry?
  I borrowed his book without asking.
- Did you forgive your friend?
  Yes, I forgave him.
- What did the teacher say?
  The teacher warned us.

- Did you both shake hands?
  Yes, we shook hands.

- Will you fight again?
  No, I will not fight again.

- Did the fight disturb the class?
  Yes, it disturbed the class.

- Why did you use bad words?
  I was very angry.

- Did your classmates stop the fight?
  Yes, they stopped it.

- Who separated you both?
  The teacher separated us.

- Did you cry after the fight?
  Yes, I cried a little.

- Was it a serious fight?
  No, it was a small fight.

- Why did you lose your temper?
  I got upset quickly.

- Did anyone get injured?
  No, nobody got injured.

- Are you friends again now?
  Yes, we are friends again.

- Did the principal call you?
  Yes, the principal called me.

- What punishment did you get?
  I got a warning.

- Did you apologize to the teacher?
  Yes, I apologized.

- Why did you throw his bag?
  I was angry at that moment.

- Did you learn anything from the fight?
  Yes, I learned to stay calm.

- Were you scared after the fight?
  Yes, I was scared.

- Did your friend insult you?
  Yes, he insulted me.

- Why did you not control your anger?
  I could not stay calm.

- Did the fight happen during break time?
  Yes, it happened during break time.

- Did your classmates support you?
  Some classmates supported me.

- What should you do instead of fighting?
  I should talk calmly.

- Did the teacher punish both of you?
  Yes, the teacher punished both of us.

- Why did you pull his shirt?
  I lost my temper.

- Did anyone complain about you?
  Yes, my friend complained.

- Did you promise not to fight again?
  Yes, I promised.

- What did your parents advise you?
  They told me to stay calm.

- Did the fight end quickly?
  Yes, it ended quickly.

- Were you punished for fighting?
  Yes, I was punished.

- What is the best way to solve problems?
  Talking calmly is the best way.

- Do you have any doubts?
  Yes, I have one doubt.

- What is your doubt?
  I did not understand the lesson.

- Can you explain this problem?
  Yes, I can explain it.

- Did you understand the question?
  No, I did not understand it.

- Which problem is difficult for you?
  Maths problems are difficult for me.

- Why are you confused?
  The question is unclear.

- Did you ask the teacher for help?
  Yes, I asked the teacher.

- Can you solve this sum?
  Yes, I can solve it.

- Why did you make this mistake?
  I misunderstood the question.

- Do you need extra practice?
  Yes, I need more practice.

- Did you read the question carefully?
  Yes, I read it carefully.

- Which answer is correct?
  The first answer is correct.

- Can you repeat the explanation?
  Yes, please repeat it.

- Did you check your answer?
  Yes, I checked it.

- Why are you worried about the test?
  I have many doubts.

- Can your friend help you?
  Yes, my friend can help me.

- Did you understand the homework?
  No, I need help.

- Which chapter gives you trouble?
  Algebra gives me trouble.

- Are you afraid to ask questions?
  No, I am not afraid.

- What should you do when you have doubts?
  I should ask the teacher.

- Did the teacher solve your problem?
  Yes, the teacher solved it.

- Why is this lesson difficult?
  It has many formulas.

- Can you explain it in simple words?
  Yes, please explain simply.

- Did you copy the notes correctly?
  No, I missed some points.

- What problem did you face in class?
  I could not hear properly.

- Can you understand English easily?
  A little.

- Why are you asking again?
  I still have confusion.

- Did you practice the problems at home?
  Yes, I practiced them.

- Which topic do you need help with?
  Algebra.

- Are you clear now?
  Yes, I am clear now.

- Did your friend explain the answer?
  Yes, he explained it well.

- Why did you leave the answer incomplete?
  I did not know the last step.

- Can you identify your mistake?
  Yes, I can identify it.

- What is the solution to this problem?
  We should divide the numbers.

- Did you understand the grammar rule?
  No, please explain again.

- Why do you find science difficult?
  The terms are hard to remember.

- Can you answer without help?
  Yes, I can try.

- What doubt do you have in English?
  I do not understand tenses.

- Can you ask your doubt confidently?
  Yes, I can ask confidently.

- Why did you skip this question?
  I did not know the answer.

- Did the example help you understand?
  Yes, it helped me a lot.

- What is confusing in this lesson?
  The explanation is confusing.

- Can you explain step by step?
  Yes, I can explain step by step.

- Did you solve the problem correctly?
  Yes, I solved it correctly.

- Why are you struggling with this chapter?
  It is very lengthy.

- Do you want another example?
  Yes, I want another example.

- Did you understand after practice?
  Yes, I understood after practice.

- What will you do if you have doubts again?
  I will ask the teacher.

24. VERB LIST

Present	Past	Past participle
Go	Went	Gone
Come	Came	Come
Do	Did	Done
Be	Was, were	Been
Play	Played	played
Teach	Taught	Taught
Spin	Spun	Spun
See	Saw	Seen
Find	Found	Found
Write	Wrote	written
Enter	Entered	Entered
Wait	Waited	Waited
Meet	Met	Met
Sit	Sat	sat
Sleep	Slept	Slept
Stand	Stood	Stood
Run	Ran	Run
Walk	Walked	Walked
Fall	Fell	Fallen
Feel	Felt	Felt

Feed	Fed	fed
Fit	Fit	Fit
Kneel	Knelt	Knelt
Keep	Kept	Kept
Knit	Knit	Knit
Miss	Missed	Missed
Bind	Bound	Bound
Tie	Tied	Tied
Tear	Tore	Torn
Eat	Ate	eaten
Speak	Spoke	Spoken
Burst	Burst	Burst
Say	Said	Said
Get	Got	Gotten
Tell	Told	Told
Throw	Threw	Thrown
Turn	Turned	Turned
Drive	Drove	Driven
Hear	Heard	Heard
Want	Wanted	Wanted
Open	Opened	Opened
Close	Closed	Closed

Ask	Asked	Asked
Talk	Talked	Talked
Pass	Passed	Passed
Save	Saved	Saved
Hold	Held	Held
Want	Wanted	Wanted
Hold	Held	Held
Cost	Cost	Cost
Sing	Sang	Sung
Sink	Sank	Sunk
Sleep	Slept	Slept
Ring	Rang	Rung
Watch	Watched	Watched
Listen	Listened	Listened
Use	Used	Used
Visit	Visited	Visited
Worry	Worried	Worried
Please	Pleased	Pleased
Hurry	Hurried	Hurried
Leave	Left	Left
Give	Gave	Given
Make	Made	Made

Drink	Drank	Drunk
Pay	Paid	Paid
Fry	Fried	Fried
Know	Knew	Known
Call	Called	Called
Cry	Cried	Cried
Win	Won	Won
Break	Broke	Broken
Take	Took	Taken
Cook	Cooked	Cooked
Begin	Began	Begun
Start	Started	Started
Warn	Warned	Warned
Study	Studied	Studied
Learn	Learnt/learned	Learnt/learned
Look	Looked	Looked
Clean	Cleaned	Cleaned
Work	Worked	Worked
Swim	Swam	Swum
Awake	Awoke	Awaken
Arise	Arose	Arisen
Type	Typed	Typed

Beat	Beat	Beaten
Become	Became	Become
Bend	Bent	Bent
Bet	Bet	Bet
Brush	Brushed	Brushed
Bite	Bit	Bitten
Bless	Blessed	Blessed
Blow	Blew	Blown
Bring	Brought	Brought
Build	Built	Built
Burn	Burnt	Burnt
Bleed	Bled	Bled
Buy	Bought	Bought
Catch	Caught	Caught
Choose	Chose	Chosen
Cling	Clung	Clung
Creep	Crept	Crept
Cut	Cut	Cut
Like	Liked	Liked
Laugh	Laughed	Laughed
Dig	Dug	Dug
Draw	Drew	Drawn

Dream	Dreamed	Dreamed
Jump	Jumped	Jumped
Fight	Fought	Fought
Flee	Fled	Fled
Fling	Flung	Flung
Fly	Flew	Flown
Forgive	Forgave	Forgiven
Forget	Forgot	Forgotten
Join	Joined	Joined
Grow	Grew	Grown
Hang	Hanged	Hanged
Hide	Hid	Hidden
Hurt	Hurt	Hurt
Hit	Hit	Hit
Lead	Led	Led
Lend	Lent	Lent
Let	Let	Let
Lose	Lost	Lost
Lay	Laid	Laid
Lie	Lied	Lied
Mow	Mowed	Mowed/mown
Put	Put	Put

Peep	Peeped	peeped
Ride	Rode	Ridden
Send	Sent	Sent
Sell	Sold	Sold
Set	Set	Set
Shake	Shook	Shaken
Shine	Shone	Shone
Shut	Shut	Shut
Spend	Spent	Spent
Pray	Prayed	Prayed
Live	Lived	Lived
Seek	Sought	Sought
Swing	Swung	Swung
Spread	Spread	Spread
Stand	Stood	Stood
Sow	Sowed	Sown
Slide	Slid	Slid
Steal	Stole	Stolen
Spin	Spun	Spun
Sting	Stung	Stung
Stink	Stank	Stunk
Spring	Sprang	Sprung

Speak	Spoke	Spoken
Wake	Woke	Woken
Wear	Wore	Worn
Weep	Wept	Wept
Wring	Wrung	Wrung
Freeze	Froze	Frozen
Have	Had	Had
Has	Had	Had
Return	Returned	Returned
Arrange	Arranged	Arranged
Remember	Remembered	Remembered
Collect	Collected	Collected
Gather	Gathered	Gathered
Assemble	Assembled	Assembled
Preside	Presided	Presided
Advise	Advised	Advised
Practise	Practised	Practised
Announce	Announced	Announced
Declare	Declared	Declared
Request	Requested	Requested
Explain	Explained	Explained
Describe	Described	Described

Appear	Appeared	Appeared
Think	Thought	Thought
Admit	Admitted	Admitted
Invite	Invited	Invited
Accept	Accepted	Accepted
Deny	Denied	Denied
Refuse	Refused	Refused
Attend	Attended	Attended
Arrive	Arrived	Arrived
Reach	Reached	Reached
Inform	Informed	Informed
Broadcast	Broadcast	Broadcast
Mistake	Mistook	Mistaken

25. TONGUE TWISTERS

- She sees cheese.
- Three tree turtles.
- He threw three balls.
- Red lorry, yellow lorry.
- Switch watch, wrist watch.
- Sheena leads, Sheila needs.
- I eat eel while you peel eel.
- Silly sheep weep and sleep.
- He threw three free throws.
- The queen in green screamed.
- What a terrible tongue twister.
- Pad kid poured curd pulled cod.
- I wish you were a fish in my dish.
- Truly rural, truly rural, truly rural.
- She sells seashells by the seashore.
- Double bubble gum, bubbles double.
- Black background, brown background.
- Shut up the shutters and sit in the shop.
- I would if I could! But I can't, so I won't!
- Which wristwatch is a Swiss wristwatch?
- Four furious friends fought for the phone.
- Peter Piper picked a peck of pickled peppers.
- I thought, I thought of thinking of thanking you.
- I scream you scream, let's all scream for ice cream!

26. PHONETICS

12 VOWELS

FRONT VOWELS

/ **i:** / - see, sea, key, police, tea, even...

/ **i** / - hit, hymn, village, sit, bit, it...

/ **e** / - bed, head, front, enter, hate, late...

/ **æ** / - sat, mad, man, batch, bad, badge...

CENTRE VOWELS

/ ʌ / - son, come, sun, cup, flood...

/ **ə:** / - bird, word, earth, first, girl...

/ **ə** / - about, abroad, above, father, the...

BACK VOWELS

/ **a:** / - passport, heart, clerk, car, bar, march...

/ **Ɔ** / - log, want, cough, gone, dog, holiday...

/ **Ɔ:** / - port, bought, law, jaw, born...

/ **u** / - pull, look, wolf, good, would, push...

/ **u:** / - pool, do, group, shoe, rule, food...

8 DIPHTHONGS

/ ei / - ape, gate, eight, aim, day, they...

/ ai / - time, life, high, island, either, buy...

/ Ɔi / - boy, oil, oyster, voice, boy, point...

/ əu / - old, home, coat, cold, wrote, foam...

/ au / - owl, out, sound, house, found, how...

/ iə / - year, here, dear, serious, near, steer...

/ uə / - poor, tour, fluent, pure, during...

/ eə / - air, bear, wear, chair, pair, their...

24 CONSONANTS

/ b / - bin, book, tub, bit, lab, sub...

/ d / - dog, rod lady, dick, pad, lead...

/ f / - fan, affair, leaf, cuff, fit, fine...

/ g / - get, again, log...

/ h / - heat, ahead, perhaps, how, hall, hat...

/ k / - cool, take, occasion, cow, call, cat...

/ l / - look, love, fool, label, allow, fellow...

/ m / - man, common, small...

/ **n** / - no, snail, knit...

/ **p** / - pin, spin, apple, pen, cup, lap...

/ **r** / - rat, very, rubber, rabbit...

/ **t** / - tea, stick, pact, tin, let, pot, set...

/ **s** / - seal, ass, cell, aside, sip, false...

/ **v** / - van, even, leave, veil, viper, verse...

/ **w** / - waste, weight, west, language, worse...

/ **θ** / - thick, breath, thigh, author, path, think....

/ **ð** / - this, thin, father, cloth, they...

/ **z** / - zeal, buzz, rose, lose, zip...

/ **ʃ** / - ship, pressure, rush, sheep, she, cash...

/ **ʒ** / - pleasure, occasion, measure...

/ **tʃ** / - church, nature, rich, chin, catch, chain...

/ **dʒ** / - magic, fridge, badge, jam, edge...

/ **ŋ** / - sing, angry, language, song, young...

/ **j** / - year, yet, yes, yawn, beyond...

27. LETTER WRITING

Leave Letter for Fever

From

S. Harini
Class VII - A
Srividyalayam Matriculation Hrs. School,
Madurai.

To

The Principal,
Srividyalayam Matriculation Hrs. School,
Madurai.

Subject: Request for two days leave.

Respected Sir,

I am a student of Class VII, Section A. I am suffering from fever and cannot attend school on 20th and 21th August 2025. Kindly grant me leave for these two days.

Yours obediently,

S. Harini
Class VII – A

Application for Transfer Certificate

From

R. Arjun
Class IX – B
St. Mary's Higher Secondary School,
Madurai.

To

The Principal,
St. Mary's Higher Secondary School,
Madurai.

Subject: Request for Transfer Certificate.

Respected Sir,

I am a student of Class IX, Roll No. 12. My father has been transferred to Chennai, so we are shifting there. Kindly issue my Transfer Certificate at the earliest to enable me to join a new school.

Yours obediently,

R. Arjun
Class IX – B

Request for Bonafide Certificate

To

The Headmaster,
Britto Matric Hrs. School,
Madurai.

Subject: Request for Bonafide Certificate.

Respected Sir,

I am a student of Class X in your school. I require a Bonafide Certificate to apply for a scholarship. Kindly issue the certificate as soon as possible.

Yours faithfully,

R. Priya
Class X – C

Sick Leave

To,

The Class Teacher,
St.Britto Matric Hrs. School
Madurai.

Respected Sir,

I am Arun, studying in class VI - B. I am not feeling well today, so I am unable to attend the class. Kindly grant me leave for one day only on 5th September 2025.
Thanking you,

Yours obediently,

Arun
Class: VI - B
Roll No: 271

Family Function Leave (2–3 Days)

To,

The Principal,
Srividyalayam Matric Hrs. School
Madurai.

Respected Madam,
I am Manikandan, a student of class VIII - B. I have to attend a family function at my hometown. Therefore, I kindly request you to grant me leave from 23 to 25 September.

I will make sure to update myself with the lessons taught during my absence.

Thanking you,

Long Leave (Medical Reason)

To,

The Principal,
Srividyalayam Matric Hrs. School,
Madurai.

Respected Madam,

I am Revathi, studying in class VII - C. I have been advised by the doctor to take complete rest as I am suffering from Asthma. Hence, I will not be able to attend school from 15 to 20th October. I kindly request you to grant me medical leave for these days.

Thanking you,

Medical Leave (3 - 4 days)

To,

The Principal,
St.Britto Matric Hrs. School
Madurai.

Respected Madam,

I am Anand, a student of Class VIII. I have been suffering from severe throat infection and the doctor has advised me to take complete rest. Therefore, I will not be able to attend school from 25 to 28. I kindly request you to grant me medical leave for these days.

I assure you that I will complete all pending assignments and classwork once I recover.

Thanking you,

Out of Station Leave (Formal & Clear)

To,

The Principal,
Srividyalayam Matric Hrs. School
Madurai.

Respected Madam,

With due respect, I would like to inform you that I will be travelling out of station with my parents for some unavoidable personal reasons. Therefore, I request you to kindly grant me leave from 25 to 28 October 2025.

I shall sincerely compensate for the missed lessons after returning to school.

Yours faithfully,

Letter to a Friend Inviting to a Birthday Party

Your Address:

23, Green Street,
Chennai – 600045.
Date: 15 November 2025.

Dear Ramesh,

I hope you are doing well. I am writing to invite you to my birthday party on 20th November at my home. The party will start at 6 p.m., and we will have games, music, and dinner.

I am looking forward to seeing you there.

Please come and make the day more special.

Yours lovingly,

Letter to the Principal – Request for Leave

From

S. Priya
Class VI B
SPV Matric Hrs. School,
Madurai.

To

The Principal,
SPV Matric Hrs. School,
Madurai.

Subject: Request for two days' leave.

Respected Sir,

I am a student of Class IX, Section B. I request you to kindly grant me leave for two days (15 and 16 August) as I am unwell. I will submit my medical certificate when I return.

I kindly request your approval.

Yours obediently,

S. Priya
Class VI B

RULES OF GOOD SPORTSMANSHIP

- Keep the playground clean.
- Line up in an orderly manner.
- Listen to the instructions.
- When the coach speaks, pay attention.
- Follow directions and safety rules.
- Be safe at all time.
- Remove jewelry, specifically watches, bracelets, rings etc.
- Don’t touch equipment without permission.
- Take care of all equipments.
- Return what you take.
- Be a good sport.
- Encourage others.
- Treat everyone with respect.
- Cooperate with others.
- Always play fairly.
- Play safe and in control.
- Learn the skills to play well.
- Stick to the rules of the game.
- Say sorry if you make a mistake.
- Learn from your mistakes.
- Have fun and do your best.
- Know how to implement strategy during games.
- When you hear the whistle, stop and listen.
- Obey the referee.
- Always give your best effort.
- Be kind when you lose.
- If you win, be a good sport.
- If you lose, practice harder.

- Lose with dignity.
- Win with class.

SCIENCE LAB SAFETY RULES

- No horseplay.
- Follow all instructions carefully.
- Learn how to use equipment.
- Use lab equipment appropriately.
- Keep your voices low so that you can hear instructions.
- Remain in your assigned area.
- Work quietly.
- No shorts or loose clothing.
- Know where safety equipment is.
- Wear safety goggles when required.
- Wear hand gloves.
- Always tie back loose hair.
- No food or drink in the lab.
- Be careful around glassware.
- Read the labels on chemicals and heed all warnings.
- Read all procedures before beginning.
- Keep electrical cords away from water.
- Put cords in a safe place.
- Be aware of open flames.
- Be careful when cutting.
- Use tongs or a mitt when handling hot materials.
- Wear an apron when working with chemicals.
- Never look directly into a test tube or flask.
- Report any accidental spills, breaking glassware, Injuries, fire, immediately.

- Never enter a science lab without a teacher in the room.
- Never take anything from the science lab without permission.
- Dispose of chemicals according to instructions.
- Do not write on the tables.
- Keep your work area clean and tidy.
- Put rubbish in the bin.
- Wash your hands after an experiment.
- No excuse for unsafe behavior in a science class.
- Everyone is responsible.

Often Used Sentences in Classroom

- May I come in, madam?
- I apologize for being late today.
- Could you please repeat the instructions?
- I didn't quite understand this concept.
- May I attempt this question?
- I'd like to correct my answer.
- Could you explain it in simpler terms?
- I have a doubt regarding this topic.
- I'll make a note of that.
- Should we write this in our notebooks?
- I have completed the assigned task.
- I need a little more time to finish this.
- May I borrow a pen, please?
- I forgot to bring my textbook.
- Could you please check my work?
- I'll submit it by tomorrow.
- I am not confident about this answer.
- I'll make sure to revise this.

- Thank you for the explanation.
- Should we underline the keywords?
- I missed the previous class.
- Could you guide me on this question?
- I'll improve my handwriting.
- May I read the next paragraph?
- I understand it much better now.
- Could you please slow down?
- I'll practice this at home.
- Is this coming for the exam?
- I appreciate your help, madam.
- I'll pay more attention.
- I need clarification on this point.
- I agree with your explanation.
- I'd like to give it a try.
- This example made it clear.
- I was confused earlier.
- I've written the answer neatly.
- Could you mark my attendance?
- I'll be more careful next time.
- What's the next period?
- Have you finished the homework?
- Let's revise together.
- Can you explain this answer?
- I missed yesterday's lesson.
- That question was tricky.
- I think the test went well.
- I ran out of time.
- Let's discuss the chapter.

- I found this topic interesting.
- Can you share your notes?
- I'm feeling confident today.
- I need help with maths.
- The syllabus is quite lengthy.
- Let's sit in the front row.
- I'll catch up soon.
- I agree with your point.
- I have a different opinion.
- Let's practice after school.
- That was a smart answer.
- I need to improve my grammar.
- I was nervous during the test.
- Let's manage our time better.
- I forgot the formula.
- That explanation helped a lot.
- I'll revise tonight.
- The exam was easier than expected.
- I'm satisfied with my performance.
- I made a silly mistake.
- I learned something new today.
- Let's not waste time.
- I'll focus more from now on.
- That chapter is important.
- I'm done with my work.
- Let's clear our doubts.
- I'm preparing seriously.
- This topic requires concentration.
- I strongly believe in hard work.

- I partially agree with this view.
- I respect your opinion.
- I see your point.
- I have a different perspective.
- This issue needs attention.
- I'd like to share my thoughts.
- I support this idea.
- I disagree for this reason.
- This decision affects everyone.
- We should stay focused.
- This habit is beneficial.
- We must think logically.
- We should be responsible.
- This topic is relevant.
- I'd like to conclude here.
- This example proves my point.
- I agree to some extent.
- This needs improvement.
- I'll begin with an introduction.
- The main theme of this chapter is…
- This lesson teaches us a moral.
- The author highlights an issue.
- I'll explain with an example.
- This answer is based on facts.
- I'd like to add one point.
- To conclude my answer…
- This topic is well explained.
- The summary is as follows.
- I've prepared thoroughly.

- I'm confident about this topic.
- I'll answer to the best of my ability.
- This diagram explains the process.
- The result shows improvement.
- The objective of this experiment is…
- The conclusion is clear.
- This data supports the theory.
- I'll speak clearly and confidently.
- I practiced several times.
- This presentation improved my confidence.
- I welcome your questions.
- Thank you for listening patiently.
- This topic required research.
- I referred to my textbook.
- I followed the instructions.
- The explanation is accurate.
- This answer is precise.
- I avoided unnecessary details.
- I structured my answer well.
- I maintained proper timing.
- This question tested understanding.
- I stayed calm during the exam.
- I reviewed my answers.
- I managed my time wisely.
- I attempted all questions.
- I avoided guesswork.
- I wrote legibly.
- I'm satisfied with my effort.
- Excuse me for the interruption.

- I truly appreciate it.
- I’m grateful for your guidance.
- I’ll be careful next time.
- I respect your decision.
- I’ll follow the rules.
- I’ll give my best effort.
- I am open to feedback.
- I’ll work on my weaknesses.
- This experience taught me a lot.
- I’m willing to learn.
- I accept my mistake.
- I’ll correct it immediately.
- I value your advice.
- I’ll stay consistent.
- I’m improving gradually.
- I’ll remain positive.
- This habit is productive.
- I’m focused on my goals.
- I’ll manage my priorities.
- I’m committed to learning.
- I’ll stay disciplined.
- I’ll not repeat this mistake.
- I’m proud of my progress.
- I’ll keep practicing.
- I’m confident in myself.
- I’m ready to face challenges.
- I’ll make better choices.
- I’ll stay motivated.
- I’m responsible for my actions.

- I'll use my time wisely.
- I'm determined to succeed.
- I believe I can improve every day.

Subject	Verb Present	Verb Past
I	am	was
He	is	was
She	is	was
It	is	was
We	are	were
You	are	were
They	are	were
He	has	had
She	has	had
It	has	had
I	have	had
We	have	had
You	have	had
They	have	had
I	do	did
We	do	did
You	do	did
They	do	did
He	does	did
She	does	did
It	does	did

www.ingramcontent.com/pod-product-compliance
Lightning Source LLC
Chambersburg PA
CBHW062136160726
48282CB00027B/846
* 9 7 8 8 1 9 9 5 4 6 8 8 2 *